"Here is a book that explores what Jesus meant when he told us we need to become as little children. With her great wealth of stories, Grace Moyer Frounfelker shares, in a simple and yet profound way, what it means to grow in childlike and Christlike qualities, which should characterize our lives.

"Many of her stories not only illustrate the childlike qualities we need but also help us realize and appreciate them in each child we meet. The book is written with warmth and love, speaks to the heart, and gently urges us to become as little children."
—*John M. Drescher, Harrisonburg, Virginia, Author,* Seven Things Children Need, *and many other books*

"This inspiring collection of true stories of children's experiences of God offers two gifts: a fresh, unsentimental view of the faith of children and an invitation to adults to open themselves again to the simplicity and joy of childlike trust in a gracious God.

"The book would be a welcome gift for parents or grandparents. It might also put a sparkle back into the eyes of tired teachers or pastors in the church. With the well-written discussion questions for each chapter, adult faith nurture groups could profit from it.

"Not weighted down with psychology (but aware of its contributions), the book stays focused on the heart of the matter: Jesus calls us to become as little children and thus receive the kingdom of God."
—*Marlene Kropf, Associated Mennonite Biblical Seminary, Elkhart, Indiana*

As a Little Child

Grace Moyer Frounfelker

Herald
Press

HERALD PRESS
Scottdale, Pennsylvania
Waterloo, Ontario

Library of Congress Cataloging-in-Publication Data
Frounfelker, Grace Moyer, 1920-
   As a little child / Grace Moyer Frounfelker.
      p. cm.
   Includes bibliographical references.
   ISBN 0-8361-9089-0 (alk. paper)
   1. Spirituality. 2. Children—Religious life. I. Title
BV4509.5.F76   1998
248.4—dc21   98-23543

The paper used in this publication is recycled and meets the
minimum requirements of the American National Standard for
Information Sciences—Permanence of Paper for Printed Library
Materials, ANSI Z39.48-1984.

Scripture is used by permission, all rights reserved, and unless
otherwise noted is from the *New Revised Standard Version Bible*,
copyright 1989, by the Division of Christian Education of the
National Council of the Churches of Christ in the USA; NEB,
from *The New English Bible*, © The Delegates of the Oxford
University Press and the Syndics of the Cambridge University
Press 1961, 1970.

07 06 05 04 03 02 01 00 99 98 10 9 8 7 6 5 4 3 2 1

*To the children
who have been my teachers*

Contents

Foreword

As a Little Child is a book after my own heart! It's about children, their spirituality, the ways they teach adults, and their ministry to adults. We are called to become like little children if we want to enter the kingdom of God.

I spent a delightful afternoon with a ten-month-old child. That evening my journalizing included the wonder of this child, Madeline Rose: *spontaneity* in laughter, *wonder* over singing birds, *amazement* in the touch of rough rain troughs or soft peony petals, *creativity and delight* with swishing water, *awe* over the accomplishment of reaching for a treasure, *pure joy* with the discovery of a kitty's tail or rough tree bark, *enjoyment* with a soft lap, a hug, and a book.

The next day, I read these stories of wonder and delight, courage and pain. Page after page added to an inspiring view of children, one that I know and share, believe and experience. I had found a kindred spirit in the author, Grace Moyer Frounfelker!

I give thanks to God for this book. It is important both to people who resonate with this perspective and others longing to understand and learn from children.

In my experiences as a teacher in church and public schools, a curriculum specialist, a parent, and a grandparent, I find people everywhere who want to be better parents and better teachers. Seldom does that wish include the realization that when we open ourselves to learn from children, we do become better teachers and parents.

As a Little Child is based on Jesus' teachings. "Unless you become as a little child," said Jesus, "you cannot enter the kingdom of God." Over and over, this scriptural nugget, aimed at adults, is intertwined with the life experiences of children. I was amazed to discover so many fresh perspectives as I absorbed that Scripture in light of children's creativity, prayer, awe and wonder, and the other chapter emphases.

In addition, we can learn from the other references to children in the Bible. Three times Samuel listens before Eli affirms that he is hearing God's voice. A little girl shows great compassion for Naaman, her captor, in wanting him to be healed of his disease.

Frounfelker has deep understandings and respect for children. She eloquently portrays children and their experiences. Children hold a unique place in God's kingdom. They surprise us with their spiritual insights, from which we can learn.

I developed a list of childlike qualities that I want to emulate, and you also may wish to do so:

- unself-conscious spontaneity
- unbounded imagination that allows freer access to the world of God's Spirit
- the ability and capacity to live in the physical and the nonphysical worlds at the same time
- seeing life and the world with a spirit of wonder,

curiosity, and awe
- having the capacity to be simple, spontaneous, and aware
- practicing compassion with innate sensitivity
- enjoying creativity that is both delightful and astounding with its seriousness and depth

This book is for people who sometimes forget to laugh *and* for those who need to learn how deeply serious children can be.

I was enchanted with Lois's imaginary playmate Frog, with the boy who cleaned up his dresser top to give center space to the baby Jesus figure from the Advent set, with the child who whispered in church as the sermon reached a crescendo, "Is this the grand finale?" (like fireworks).

In our hurried and harried grown-up worlds, some folks equate success with sophistication, seriousness, and organization. The stories tickled my funny bone. They kept me reading and wanting more.

At the same time that the book made me smile, it also gave me a glimpse into the wisdom of children. The insights they share, the compassion they show— these are ways we must learn to "enter the kingdom."

There was an authentic and compelling quality as I read. Frounfelker has recorded verbatim conversations, learnings, and reflections from children. This approach is filled with integrity and encourages me to keep recording and remembering my own astounding experiences with children.

Especially meaningful to me personally is the gift

of imagination that children give us, as described in various parts of the book. Too often we have discredited this gift from God.

I appreciate the wealth of quotes from outstanding and respected authors, such as Paul Tournier, Richard Foster, Morton Kelsey, Henry Nouwen, Thomas Merton. These readings add credibility to the true stories about children, the quotes from the Bible, and the author's personal insights.

All kinds of subliminal teaching tips await our discovery here. As we adults begin truly to listen to children, we can discover many ways to learn from them, relate to them, and care for them better.

This book is a treasure, filled with tidbits on the art of asking questions, perceiving unmet needs, catching glimpses into children's lives as they talk, and reflecting deeply on the meaning of what children say or do or share.

As a Little Child motivates me to spend more time with the children in my congregation, all the *Jubilee* children I know, my youngest grandchild Madeline Rose, and my next grandchild, whom we await. The book inspires me to face life like a child, to learn from the children, and to respond to Jesus Christ with the spontaneous joy of a child.

As you read, I hope your response is similar.

—*Rosella Wiens Regier*
   Executive Director, Jubilee: God's Good News
   Newton, Kansas

Preface

Jesus was indignant! Indignant with whom? With disciples who tried to drive away people bringing little children to him. Jesus took those little children into his arms, laid his hands on them, and blessed them.

He said to his disciples, "It is to such as these that the kingdom of God belongs. . . . Whoever does not receive the kingdom of God as a little child will never enter it" (Mark 10:13-16).

Not only in this instance did Jesus demonstrate the unique place of children in his kingdom. His disciples came questioning, "Who is the greatest in the kingdom of heaven?"

Jesus called a child, whom he put among them, and said, "Truly I tell you, unless you change and become like children, you will never enter the kingdom of heaven. Whoever becomes humble like this child is the greatest in the kingdom of heaven" (Matt. 18:1-4).

Paul said that when he became a man, he put away childish things. But Jesus had said, become like children. Do these statements contradict each other? No, because Jesus was talking about childlikeness, and Paul about childishness.

The dictionary says that "childlike and childish are both applied to persons of any age in referring to characteristics or qualities considered typical of a child; childlike suggesting the favorable qualities such as innocence, guilelessness, trustfulness, etc., and childish, the unfavorable, as immaturity, foolishness, petulance, etc."

As I grow in Christian maturity, have I disdained the behaviors of children? Have I lost the childlike along with discarding the childish?

Children seem naturally at home in the world of God's Spirit, the kingdom of God within and around us.

As I have lived with children and taught them, they have often surprised me with insights far beyond my expectations. I presumed that I was the teacher. Nevertheless, they were teaching me. So this is not a book about how we teach children. It is about how children teach us!

Much that I relate in this book is from personal experience. Family and friends have shared some with me. A few names have been changed to protect privacy.

I believe that the children whose stories I tell are not atypical children. Instead, they express the spiritual potential of every child who has not been too negatively impacted by our culture. Thus they also express the spiritual potential of every adult Christian who seeks to become childlike.

—*Grace Moyer Frounfelker*
Bluffton, Ohio

The Spiritual Life
of the Child

CHRISTINE, less than four years old, ran into the kitchen. "Mommy, do you know that Jesus died on the cross and then he came alive again and hopped right down? And now he's here beside me all the time." She held out her right hand. "And over here on this side is my angel." She extended her left hand.

Before her astonished mother could respond, Christine called joyfully, "Come on, you guys!" Beckoning with both hands, she ran outdoors to play, accompanied, without doubt, by Jesus and her angel.

Jesus said, "Out of the mouths of infants and nursing babies you have prepared praise for yourself" (Matt. 21:16). With the unself-conscious spontaneity of a child, Christine was expressing her perception of God, her awareness of the world of the Spirit, the kingdom Jesus came to proclaim.

Twelve adult men, accompanying Jesus for three

years, could not grasp this until after his resurrection.

Both followers and critics of Jesus were looking for a visible kingdom of political power and earthly muscle. They wanted a king who would drive out the Romans and end Israel's subjection, a descendant of David who would reign from Jerusalem, the capital.

They had heard John the Baptist proclaim, "Repent, for the kingdom of heaven has come near" (Matt. 3:1-2). When John was imprisoned, Jesus repeated that same message (Matt. 4:17). The Pharisees apparently had this Davidic kingdom in mind when they confronted Jesus and asked when the kingdom of God would come.

"The kingdom of God is not coming with things that can be observed," Jesus explained. "Nor will they say, 'Look, here it is!' or 'There it is!' For, in fact, the kingdom of God is among you" (Luke 17:20-21).

They didn't grasp it. Out of earshot of Jesus, the disciples argued about which of them would be greatest in the kingdom. They didn't win followers by flaunting their own credentials, arguing about their own qualifications for leadership.

Even Mrs. Zebedee got into the act. She asked that Jesus would award to her sons, James and John, the seats of honor at his right hand and at his left. The ten disciples were indignant with the Zebedee brothers.

Patiently Jesus explained that he and his kingdom would not follow the way of world rulers. "Whoever wishes to be great among you must be your servant, and whoever wishes to be first among you must be your slave" (Matt. 20:20-28).

Jesus calls for us to become as a little child, to be a servant, a slave. With these words, Jesus paved the way into the world of the Spirit, his kingdom.

Jesus planned a last sacred evening alone with his disciples before his crucifixion. "I have eagerly desired to eat this Passover with you before I suffer; for I tell you, I will not eat it until it is fulfilled in the kingdom of God. . . . This is my body, which is given for you. . . . This cup that is poured out for you is the new covenant in my blood."

In these solemn moments, how could the disciples again start quibbling about who was to be the greatest in the kingdom? "The kings of the Gentiles lord it over them; and those in authority over them are called benefactors. But not so with you," Jesus reminded them. "Rather the greatest among you must become like the youngest, and the leader like one who serves" (Luke 22:14-27).

As we believers partake of the Lord's Supper, do we remember these words of Jesus? Jonathan, Christine's four-year-old brother, and his family were attending a church that observed the Lord's Supper every second Sunday. One Sunday Jonathan asked, "Mom, why do you people do that?"

"We eat the little piece of bread and drink the grape juice because Jesus told us to do it to remember him," whispered his mother.

Jonathan appeared satisfied with the answer, and his mother said no more. Weeks later, after he had witnessed several more observances of the Lord's Supper, he commented again. "Mom, you grown-ups have to go up there and eat to remember Jesus. But I don't need to 'cause I don't never forget him."

I want to live with this childlike awareness of the spiritual kingdom that lets me say with Jonathan, "I don't never forget him."

If I want to go beyond Christian maturity, into childlikeness, I am faced with some hard questions. What is the beginning of spiritual awareness for the child? At what point in life is God first aware of the child and the child's spiritual potential?

The Lord assured Jeremiah, "Before I formed you in the womb I knew you, and before you were born I consecrated you; I appointed you a prophet to the nations" (Jer. 1:4-5). The psalmist was sure that the Lord was aware of him as an unborn child.

It was you who formed my inward parts;
     you knit me together in my mother's womb.
. . . I am fearfully and wonderfully made.
Wonderful are your works; that I know very well.
My frame was not hidden from you,
     when I was being made in secret,
     intricately woven in the depths of the earth.
Your eyes beheld my unformed substance.
In your book were written
     all the days that were formed for me,
     when none of them as yet existed.

                               (Ps. 139:13-16)

Yes, the Lord knows the unborn child. Is it possible that the unborn child also is aware of the Lord?

Elizabeth, mother of John the Baptist, tells us that her unborn child responded with spiritual awareness. Mary, fresh from the revelation that she was to be the mother of the Messiah, went to visit her kinswoman.

Six months pregnant, Elizabeth spoke for both herself and the child in her womb when she responded to Mary's greeting.

"Blessed are you among women, and blessed is the fruit of your womb. And why has this happened to me, that the mother of my Lord comes to me? For as soon as I heard the sound of your greeting, the child in my womb leaped for joy" (Luke 1:39-45).

The unborn child can at least perceive sound and distinguish between sounds. I know two preschool children who could carry a tune and were singing almost as soon as they were speaking. Both mothers are church organists.

One child at age five picked out tunes on a simple stringed instrument. Both children in the womb heard their mothers play organ or piano almost daily. As tiny babies, they accompanied mothers to organ lessons and practice.

Elissa, age three, and her mother arrived early for mother's lesson. Mother set a few stops on the huge organ and allowed Elissa to press some keys. The child touched some low notes and said, "That sounds like big, strong angels." She slid to the other end of the keyboard, touched some high notes, and said, "That sounds like little, tiny, happy angels."

Elissa's mother told me that when she was eight months pregnant, she was singing with the famous Bach Choir of Bethlehem, Pennsylvania. They were rehearsing Handel's *Messiah* with orchestra accompaniment. She became aware that the baby responded with excited movement whenever the brasses played. The choir member seated next to her also noticed the baby's movements.

Christian music was part of the lives of these children from conception. I believe that conditioning enhances their world of the Spirit.

A young couple, I'll call them Jan and Jim, began a bedtime devotional discipline when they were married. When Jan became pregnant, they included the child in their family devotions. They joined hands to pray and each placed a free hand on Jan's abdomen, creating a family circle of love and prayer.

One evening they came home late and tired, and decided to skip the devotional time and go to sleep. But sleep eluded Jan. The baby moved restlessly. Jan's head throbbed. Finally she woke her husband.

"Please, let's have our Bible reading and prayer. I believe we need it, the baby and I." Together they read and prayed. The baby quieted. The whole family slipped into a night of peaceful rest.

So we see how such things may impact the unborn child: the voice of Mary, mother of Jesus; the beauty of Christian music; and parents in prayer.

The more I learn from children's expressions of

spirituality, the more I see such instances as Jesus' small miracles of instruction, teaching me what he meant when he told us to become childlike. They are not merely coincidences. I heard someone say, A coincidence is God's way of performing a miracle while remaining anonymous.

Paul Tournier wrote, "The child is not an empty sack to be filled with all the things that adults have learned and things they think, but a sack quite full of treasures already."[1]

Jesse was about five years old when he was helping his father arrange the nativity scene in the living room. "What's so great about this whole thing," marveled Jesse, "is that these people *really* lived and this story *really* happened!"

Albert Edward Day, founder of the Disciplined Order of Christ, shares a treasure from his own childhood. At age six in the church his grandfather pastored, he went forward when an altar call was given. He says that no one came to counsel with him. Maybe they thought he was too young; maybe no one there knew how to deal with so young a child. He was left alone.

So all by himself, the child told Jesus about what he perceived as his sins. He asked for forgiveness. He says, "Christ seemed to be standing there before me, in the white purity of his adorable Presence, saying to me, 'Thy sins are forgiven.' "[2]

The memory of that vision did not fade, says Day. No one had told him that a child might expect such an experience. But the reality of it stayed with him all through his life.

If a child in the womb may be spiritually impacted, more certainly may the child at age four or six. As we recognize the spiritual awareness of the small child, we may recall experiences from our own childhood. It will encourage us to move more deeply into experiences of childlikeness as adults.

To Be Childlike

1. What is your definition of "childlike"? What are the attributes of a childlike Christian? Write your thoughts in a journal (as though recording a journey, one with a goal in view).

2. What are your own spiritual goals? Which of these are consistent with the definition you wrote?

3. Do you need visual reminders to help you invite the Lord Jesus to be your constant companion through the day? A picture, motto, or Bible verse on your desk, the car dashboard, or the refrigerator door? Record the symbol that you choose. Jesus will be delighted to hear you say frequently to him and to your angel, as Christine did, "Come on, you guys!"

4. What contacts do you have with children in your neighborhood or church, with your own children or grandchildren? Plan some activity with them that will give you opportunities to listen and learn.

5. Can you, like Albert Day, open yourself to God in childlike sincerity? Can you trust God to be present to you in new, unexpected ways?

Living in the World of the Spirit

FOR about two years I cared for my niece two days a week. She was three to four years old. Not long after we began this close relationship, Lois opened a kitchen closet door and invited Frog to come out and play with us. From that time on, Frog accompanied everything that she did at my home.

When her father came to pick her up, her last act was to open the closet door so Frog could return to his waiting place. The next time she came, she opened the closet door to greet Frog, even before she removed her coat. I accepted Frog as a part of all our days together.

Donny, a neighbor child Lois's age, came occasionally to play with her. Donny could not accept Frog. He and Lois played house. Their children were Lois's dolls, a clown that sprang out of a musical jack-in-the-box, and Frog. Donny appealed to me. "Tell her she mayn't talk to Frog. There isn't any Frog!"

I tried to explain that Frog was a make-believe friend. "He can be your friend too, Donny. You can pretend Frog is here; you can talk with him. Or would you like to have a pretend friend of your own? You can have any pretend friend you would like to have."

I was wrong. Poor Donny couldn't! He had a temper tantrum because I didn't force Lois to deny or dismiss Frog. I felt great sadness for Donny. I realized that his home training stressed truthfulness, with truth defined as only what we experience through our five senses. Fairy tales were forbidden. It cost Donny a treasured part of childhood, in imagination and creativity, and I suspect also in spirituality.

Years later I heard that Donny was now a schoolteacher and had moved out of our area. When we met one day in late autumn, I asked if he had taken a different job.

"Yes," he replied, "I'm going to be married next month, and we decided to settle here in our hometown."

I had been married only a year earlier. I tried to express my own great joy in my marriage relationship, and I wished for him that his marriage would be similarly fulfilling.

"Oh, I've been careful and taken my time," he said. "I know this will be right. She sews all her own clothes and bakes great sticky buns."

I looked for the twinkle in his eye that said he was

sharing a joke with me. There was none! I walked away with a heavy feeling that he was still missing much more than an imaginary Frog.

Morton Kelsey states a basic viewpoint of Jesus: he "undoubtedly believed that there were two interacting dimensions of reality, physical and nonphysical, both created by God and both good."[1]

Small children live much of their awareness in that nonphysical world. When we live close to children, we are blessed whenever they invite us inside that world, to view it from the child's perspective.

Kelsey admits, "It is not easy for mature people to grasp this idea of two ways of experiencing and knowing, and of two areas or realms that can be known. Children, however, can get it quite easily since they have not been conditioned into believing that the realm of sense experience and physicality is all that exists. . . . Human beings are not confined to a physical world."[2]

The happy child who is permitted and encouraged to develop imagination, to live with companions like Frog, has freer access to the world of the spirit, and to be in touch with God's Spirit. Like Christine (in chapter 1), such a child more readily senses and accepts spiritual presence in her life. This may be the presence of Jesus, or of her angel.

In addition to Frog, Lois gave me many more glimpses into her ability to live in two worlds. On an autumn walk through a nearby park, I would have stepped on a line of ants if she had not warned me.

We stopped to watch them scurry from a discarded bread crust to their hole in the ground, each carrying a crumb.

We talked about their storeroom for the winter when there would be no more picnics in the park. We picked up red and yellow and brown leaves. We watched clouds like flocks of sheep moving across the sky. We marveled at a perfectly patterned spiderweb.

When we came home, I prepared lunch. Lois attended to her doll family. She lulled them to sleep with a song she composed: "Dear Heavenly Father, kind and good, thank you for the green grass we walk on all the time. . . ."

We had not talked about God during our walk. Lois's material and spiritual worlds were so integrated that she turned naturally to thank the heavenly Father for the simple joys of the morning. On another occasion, I was happy to have paper and pencil nearby when I heard her sing as she busied herself with paper and crayons.

Jesus died for all the people.
I love him. I love him.
Jesus died for all the children.
Jesus died. Jesus died.

Jesus died for all the people
'cause God is great.
Please him, please him
For all blessings.

For God is rose now from the dead.
God is great now, well and good.
He's strong like he was.
He's strong like he was.

Because children live easily in that nonphysical world, I believe they are open to experiences in the world of the spirit and of God's Spirit. What we adults strive for seems to come naturally to them.

Sophia was less than three years old when her mother came into her bedroom some time after putting her to bed. The child lay quietly awake.

"What are you doing, Sophia?" asked her mother.

"I talking with Jesus," she replied.

"What did Jesus say to you?"

"He say, 'Thank you for the visit.' "

No doubt Jesus and Sophia had been conversing.

One Sunday morning, Terrence, a ten-year-old boy in my church school class, gave me a glimpse into a Holy Place in his spiritual world. Each Sunday morning I picked up Terrence and three preschoolers at the home where they were foster children. As we drove to church, we paused for a traffic light and saw people entering another church. Bruce asked, "Is Jesus in that church?"

"Yes," I assured him, "Jesus is in that church, and he is also in our church. Jesus is with us always, when we are in church, or at home, or in the car, or anywhere."

I repeated Bruce's question as an opener in my class with Terrence and the other children that morning. We were beginning a series titled What Is God Like? I reported that many people, like little Bruce, have asked, "Can I see God? What is God like?"

"When we see a photo," I continued, "or meet a new person, that alone does not tell us what that person is like. The Bible tells us what Jesus did and what he taught. So we begin to see that Jesus is loving, caring, kind. God is like Jesus. That is the most important way we know what God is like."

During this introduction I noticed that Terrence seemed distracted, disturbed about something. He started to speak, hesitated, stammered, and said, "No, I can't tell because you wouldn't believe me."

I assured him that when we want to share something important, we look for people we can trust. It was all right if he didn't feel ready to trust us with what was bothering him. I continued with my lesson.

Terrence again asked to tell about something that had happened. He proceeded hesitantly, stumbling over words. His foster home included two teenage girls in addition to the four I brought to church.

On Saturday the foster mother had gone away for awhile and left the two girls in charge. Each child was supposed to clean his or her room. Terrence defied the girls. To punish him, they dragged him into the basement and locked him in an inner basement room without a window or a light switch.

"I was really scared, and I prayed," he told us.

Halting, searching for words, Terrence described how a soft light began to glow at the far end of the room. In that light, he saw a person with his back turned toward him. He saw the top part of the figure to the waist. Although he did not see the person's face, he knew that the person was the Lord Jesus. Then the light slowly faded, and darkness enveloped him again.

The children stared wide-eyed. The teacher breathed a silent prayer for HELP.

"How did you feel then, Terrence?" I asked.

"I wasn't afraid anymore."

For me, that reply validated his experience. The other children in my class expressed wonder, belief, trust, and spiritual excitement.

As I pondered Terrence's experience, I remembered Moses in the wilderness after the Israelites had made the golden calf. The Lord had assured Moses that Moses was known by name, and that the Lord had promised, "I will go with you." Still, Moses sought further proof. He prayed that he might see the Lord's glory.

"You cannot see my face; for no one shall see me and live. . . . See, there is a place by me where you shall stand on the rock; and while my glory passes by I will put you in the cleft of the rock, and I will cover you with my hand until I have passed by; then I will take away my hand, and you shall see my back; but my face shall not be seen" (Exod. 33:12-23).

I talked with a trusted Christian friend about Terrence's vision. She listened intently and then told me of a similar experience. She rarely told others of her vision, she said, because people tended to set her apart as "holier than thou." But it had come at a crisis time when she might have moved away from God.

She, too, had seen the light, the figure only to the waist, the face turned away, and felt the certainty that she was in the presence of Jesus.

I thrill to know that the God of Moses, the God of a beautiful Christian friend, is also the God of a scared little boy in a dark basement.

Why have I never had a visible glimpse into the spiritual world? I pondered that again after a weekly Bible study with adults. We met in the basement of a home, a room lighted by a single bare lightbulb overhead.

One woman was emotionally shattered as she started telling details of an unbelievably damaged childhood. I sat beside her, put my arms around her, and the group joined me in prayer for the healing presence of Jesus upon that devastated little child within.

I asked the woman to let herself remember the childhood home, to let herself be the frightened little girl in the dismal kitchen. I prayed that the Lord Jesus would come and knock at the door, and suggested that the little girl invite him to come in. Then we sat in silence. I don't know how long we all supported her in silent prayer.

I felt the woman relax in my arms. She spoke. She said that the Lord Jesus had come into the room, sat in the rocking chair, and held her in his arms. Then he told her to go and play, and he would like to watch.

Play? As the oldest of eight children, with alcoholic parents, she never had time to play. Jesus wanted her just to play, and he smiled as he watched her.

As the childhood scene faded, the woman opened her eyes and looked around the room. "Oh, it's so bright in here! I can hardly stand the brightness!"

Her remark held no significance for me until later. One of our group members had arrived late. As she started down the basement stairs, she saw that we were all in silent prayer. She sat down on the top step and waited. After the meeting she told our hostess that through all the time of silence, a bright light hovered over the heads of the group seated below her at the table. It gradually faded as the prayer time ended.

For the devastated woman, the events of the evening were the start of her journey toward spiritual and physical healing.

When alone, I thought things over. Why hadn't I seen the light? Why do others have such experiences in my presence, and I don't see anything?

The answer I received was much like the one that Jesus gave to Thomas, who needed to see and touch the risen Lord before he could believe. Jesus said, "Have you believed because you have seen me? Blessed are those who have not seen and yet have come to believe" (John 20:24-29).

That distressed woman needed the visual sign, the blinding light when she opened her eyes. The woman sitting on the stairs validated that sign. Perhaps the woman on the stairs needed it, too. I don't know. I am assured, however, that I can live in the world of the Spirit as confidently as if I have seen visual signs.

The apostle Paul seemed to live easily in the reality of the spiritual world. He addressed the Ephesians,

> Blessed be the God and Father of our Lord Jesus Christ, who has blessed us in Christ with every spiritual blessing in the heavenly places. . . . I pray that the God of our Lord Jesus Christ, the Father of glory, may give you a spirit of wisdom and revelation as you come to know him, so that, with the eyes of your heart enlightened, you may know . . . what is the immeasurable greatness of his power for us who believe. (Eph. 1:3, 17-19)

If we want to learn from children the qualities of childlikeness, we need to approach with humility the spirituality of children. Can we as rational adults recover that ease of living in the awareness of these spiritual blessings that are ours in heavenly places?

Writers, both Christian and secular, confirm the exceptional ability of the child to live easily and naturally in the world of the spirit as well as the physical world.

Robert Coles, noted psychiatrist and professor at Harvard University, spent several years of research on this subject. He left the psychiatrist's office and the children labeled as needing psychiatric help. Coles sought out children in their own environments, in many countries, in a variety of cultures and religious backgrounds. He released his extensive findings in his book *The Spiritual Life of Children*.[3]

A classic in child psychology literature is *The Inner World of Childhood*, by Frances G. Wickes. In the preface she states, "It is from the children themselves that we learn, and it is from their gifts to us that we grow in understanding."

Wickes devotes a chapter to "Imaginary Companions." I saw Lois's Frog in what Wickes describes as "the imaginary playmate of a happy, much-loved child. . . . Her garden is full of children. . . . Fairies live under the big syringa bush."[4]

When children find something wonderful, they want to share it. Let me never be too busy to explore with them. They seem to be more aware of God's small miracles than we who are too preoccupied to observe.

Lois was three when she came running indoors, wide-eyed with excitement. "Come quick, Aunt Grace! Elfes live in our yard!" I dropped everything and ran with her. She had found toadstools in the grass following yesterday's rain. I remembered that several days earlier I had read to her, "Under a toadstool crept a wee elf, out of the rain to shelter himself. . . ."

With our faces down in the grass we agreed that we didn't see any "elfes" there at the moment. They didn't need the shelter in the day's warm sunshine.

The skeptic may ask, "What does God have to do with toadstools and elves?" I leave that for you to answer for yourself. Does our concept of God and

God's arena become larger or smaller as we become adults and leave childlikeness behind?

Lois is now the mother of three children, Christine and Jonathan, to whom you were introduced in the first chapter, and Naomi.

I'm thankful that at age ten Christine has not been "educated" out of awareness of the world of the spirit. She told her mother one morning that she had gone to bed feeling scared because she had read scary stories that evening.

"But I went to sleep all right because I had Jesus on one side of me and Grandma Marshall on the other side." Grandma Marshall had died when Christine was only two. Her grandchildren continue to envision her caring presence watching over them.

Lois wrote about that to me and added, "It's so hard for me as an adult to recapture that childlike faith, but I feel it's the only way." That only way is becoming, again, as a little child.

Richard Foster agrees. In his book *Celebration of Discipline*, he stresses the importance of thinking and experiencing in images.

> The inner world of meditation is most easily entered through the door of imagination. . . . It comes so spontaneously to children, but for years now we have been trained to disregard the imagination, even to fear it. . . . Just as children need to learn to think logically, adults need to rediscover the magical reality of the imagination.[5]

Author Sofia Cavalletti also describes the sensitivity children show for the world of God.

> We have attempted to document the existence of a mysterious bond between God and the child. . . . It subsists in early childhood even in cases of spiritual "malnutrition" and appears to precede any religious instruction whatsoever. The manifestations of serene and peaceful joy the children display in meeting with the world of God lead us to maintain that the religious experience responds to a deep "hunger" in the children.[6]

I was reminded of that comment about spiritually malnourished children when a family with two small sons was visiting us. I suspected that their exposure to Christian teaching was almost nonexistent.

The two boys joined me as I was in the kitchen preparing breakfast. My husband knew that as soon as he appeared, the boys, to whom we were acting grandparents, would demand all his attention. He stayed in our bedroom to have his quiet time with the Lord.

"Where's Granddad?" asked one boy.

"He's upstairs in our bedroom," I replied.

"What is he doing?" asked the child.

"He's talking with God. He likes to talk with God first thing in the morning."

"Talking with God?" questioned the older boy, seven years old. "How can somebody talk with God? Does he have God up there in his room?"

I tried to explain that God is everywhere, and that we can talk with him wherever we are.

"You mean God is here on the table? Then I can give him a karate chop if I want to!" And the older boy slammed his fist on the table.

The younger boy, perhaps four, raised his head, his face aglow with a look of surprise and wonder. "Hello, God!" he said reverently.

Dr. Diane Komp, a pediatric oncologist, teaches and practices at Yale University School of Medicine. In her book *A Window to Heaven* she tells the story of her own journey from unbelief to faith, guided by her patients, children suffering and dying from cancer. She calls them "the littlest of God's giants." She describes herself as having been somewhere between agnostic and atheist.

"Over the years," she says, "I have come to the conclusion that dramatic conversion to disbelief is rare. More often, faith dies from disuse, atrophy, a failure to be exercised. Such was my experience. . . . I decided not to attempt to find a meaning in suffering. I only sought to fight against it."

Dr. Komp tells of one dying child who saw beautiful angels and heard beautiful singing. She relates that this child and others with similar experiences brought her back to the life of faith. "Because of these children, my life has been changed and I have seen other lives changed. . . . These children have been faithful witnesses to me."[7]

I appreciate Dr. Komp's accounts of sick and dying

children. But I am thankful, also, to be a witness to spirituality in the lives of healthy, happy children.

Sophia, age four, had heard in church school about Jesus' visit to the home of Mary and Martha.

"Mom, it's better to think about God than to eat." She paused, then added, "But God made food, too. So I can eat and think about God at the same time."

A Litany for Children

> O Lord of light and Source of all creation,
>   we praise and glorify you for the children
>   you have given us.
> For their lives, their inquiring minds,
>   and receptive spirits . . .
> For their joyous ways that fill us with
>   wonder and delight . . .
> For their simple trust in you in these
>   complex and troubled times,
> We thank you, O God.[8]

To Be Childlike

1. Can you recall imaginary companions from your early childhood? Were they friends? Record these memories in your journal. They may be spiritual allies.

2. For most adults, our days are spent in the world of the senses, the physical world. What in your environment helps you to live part of this day in the world

of God's kingdom, the nonphysical world? Art? Music? Meditation?

3. Something as simple as the discipline of prayer before meals can open the door into the spiritual world. Can you envision the hands of Jesus as the host who passes the food? You could place an empty chair at the table as a sign of his presence.

4. In what ways can you use imagination to enrich your spiritual life? Paul wrote to the Ephesians, "God has bestowed on us in Christ every spiritual blessing in the heavenly places." How do you envision those heavenly places? Are they superimposed on your ordinary everyday world?

5. Can you make opportunities to listen to children share their ideas of what God is like, expressed both orally and in their art?

3

Prayer, Language of the Spiritual World

NAOMI, Lois's older daughter, was five when Grandma Marshall died. Naomi's bedtime prayer habit was to pray aloud after her parents had left the room, with just Naomi and God in conversation. Often a parent lingered in the hall to eavesdrop.

During the year that Grandma Marshall was ill, Naomi often prayed for her healing. Sometimes she was angry with God because Grandma was not getting well.

One night several weeks after Grandma's death, Lois listened as Naomi prayed her usual prayer, that God would bless Mommy and Daddy, Christine and Jonathan. Then she added, "And God, how are you and Grandma Marshall getting along?" There was a long pause. Then Naomi exclaimed, "Oh! Good!"

We adults stand in awe of the child's spiritual perception, and we need to respect the mystery. It seems natural to small children to expect an answer when they pray, as natural as a parent's spoken response. Maybe I no longer expect it and that's why my spiritual ears grow deaf.

Friends and their small daughter had gone to visit acquaintances who had moved into a new geodesic house. The next morning Elissa, age three, voiced her usual prayer of thanks for breakfast. Then she said, "I want to tell God something else." She added to her prayer, "God, I want to live in a ball house when I grow up." She looked to her parents, smiling, and exclaimed, "He said I could."

In *Celebration of Discipline*, Richard Foster cautions,

> We should never make prayer too complicated. . . . Jesus taught us to come like children to a father. Openness, honesty, and trust mark a child's communication with father. There is an intimacy between parent and child that has room for both seriousness and laughter. . . . Children teach us the value of imagination. . . . The imagination is a powerful tool in the work of prayer.[1]

I believe that God is communicating always, all around us, by many voices, spoken, written, nonverbal, symbolic, and imaginative. The want of miracle and mystery is not in God's lack of communication with us, but in our lack of capacity to perceive.

Eli, the old priest in Israel, heard nothing. "The word of the Lord was rare in those days" (1 Sam. 3:1). But the child Samuel heard the Lord calling him by

name. Is it possible that Eli was also within sound of
the Lord's voice and still was blocked from hearing?
Why?

The story in 1 Samuel suggests that Eli had given
up his responsibilities both as parent and as high
priest. He allowed his two sons to grow up without
parental discipline. The father-son relationship
reached the point where the growing sons rejected
their father's counsel.

Eli's sons were also priests, under the authority of
Eli as high priest. Yet they were sexually promiscuous
within the shadow of the tabernacle and desecrated
the sacrifices brought here. Apparently only the child
Samuel had the spiritual perception, in that time and
place, to hear the voice of the Lord.

James D. Burns describes the experience in the
words of an old hymn.

> Hushed was the evening hymn,
>   The temple courts were dark,
> The lamp was burning dim
>   Before the sacred ark;
> When suddenly a Voice divine
>   Rang through the silence of the shrine.
>
> The old man, meek and mild,
>   The priest of Israel slept;
> His watch the temple-child,
>   The little Levite kept.
> And what from Eli's sense was sealed,
>   The Lord to Hannah's son revealed.

O give me Samuel's ear:
 The open ear, O Lord,
Alive and quick to hear
 Each whisper of thy Word!
Like him to answer at thy call,
 And to obey thee first of all.

O give me Samuel's heart:
 A lowly heart that waits
Where in thy house thou art,
 Or watches at thy gates!
By day and night, a heart that still
 Moves at the breathing of thy will.

O give me Samuel's mind:
 A sweet, unmurmuring faith,
Obedient and resigned
 To thee in life and death!
That I may read with childlike eyes
 Truths that are hidden from the wise.[2]

Particularly in public prayer, how have we moved so far from the childlike simplicity of talking with a loving heavenly Parent?

Some people seem to assume that only the pastor is qualified to pray publicly. I was asked to speak one Sunday morning in a three-church charge. That meant speaking in three different churches between 8:30 and noon. I accepted on condition that a lay person in each congregation serve as worship leader.

I gave lay leaders suggestions for call to worship, prayer for the offering, and so on. Since the congregational prayer was to be in response to praises and concerns voiced by the audience, no written prayer was provided.

In the first service, the leader asked for silent prayer. In the second church, the leader invited the people to share concerns and asked them to pray the Lord's Prayer with him. The leader in the third church said, "They didn't give me anything for this prayer, so we'll skip it and sing the next hymn."

Contrast this with a scene in vacation Bible school. It was snack time, with milk and cookies waiting. The teacher asked Ollie, a chubby six-year-old, to give thanks before we ate. Ollie prayed, "God, thank ya for the good milk and cookies, and all us kids love ya. Amen."

A friend gives piano lessons to children. She told me that Carol had played through her assignment for the week without error. Just as she finished, there was a crash of thunder, and rain slammed against the window. Carol cried delightedly, "Oh, God is clapping for me!"

God claps! God directs! God consoles! God comforts and loves! I want to be alert to these many expressions of the voice of the Lord.

One time I quit a job that had become intolerable. A new manager had communicated not too subtly that he would not accept me as second in command. The next morning, I awoke with the realization that I had no job to go to, no idea of where to look for work, no assurance of the next paycheck.

I became aware that the only sound penetrating the early-morning stillness was the song of the birds. They spoke the Lord's message to me. Take no thought for what you shall eat or how you shall pay the rent. Consider the birds. Your heavenly Father feeds them. You are of more worth to me than many birds.

Did I pray? Yes, fervently. But even before a prayer in words, I heard the expression of God's caring. Within a month I was offered two positions more satisfying and fulfilling than the one I had quit.

The simplicity of children's prayers is matched by their ability to see and sense God's presence. One little boy sneezed in the middle of his prayer. He said, "Oh dear God, please excuse me for sneezing right in your face!"

Sometimes God finds ways to speak love to children even when parents may be less than perfect in trying to teach appropriate behavior. Women in our church were spending a day sewing. Pamela had brought five-year-old Tommy with her. Tommy soon tired of the toys she had brought for him. He ventured into activities that distressed his mother and the busy women.

His mother said, "Tommy, you're doing naughty things, and that makes us all unhappy. It makes Jesus unhappy, too. I want you to go into the church meeting room and sit there for awhile. And tell Jesus you're sorry."

Tommy was gone for perhaps ten or fifteen minutes. His attention was drawn to the huge stained-glass window of Jesus as the Good Shepherd, with the morning sun streaming through its brilliant colors. When he returned to the sewing room, he busied himself with his toys and activity books.

"Tommy, did you do what I asked?" questioned Pamela.

"Yes, and it's all right now."

"How do you know it's all right?" Pamela was puzzled by Tommy's calm assurance.

"Well, Jesus didn't say anything. But the little lamb he's holding wiggled its ear at me, so I know it's all right."

My own lack of faith once caused me to miss a teaching opportunity with children in my church school class. Our lesson centered on Jesus' teachings about prayer. I asked the children, "What would you like to pray about this morning?"

"Is it all right to pray for animals?" asked Natalie.

We reflected on what Jesus said about the Father's care for sparrows. "Yes, it's all right to pray for animals."

"My sister's dog had puppies yesterday, thirteen of them," related Natalie. "The vet says that's too many puppies for the mother to feed, and they won't all live. I want to pray that none of the puppies will die."

The children named other prayer needs and prayed for them all. But thirteen newborn puppies had captured the heart of the children's concerns. Each child prayed fervently that the puppies would live and thrive.

I approached the following Sunday with anxiety. Would the children ask about the puppies? How would we handle it if even one puppy had died? I breathed easier when the class ended and no one had asked about the puppies.

Several weeks later, I met Natalie's big sister. Casually I asked, "How is your litter of puppies coming along?"

"They are growing and thriving, all thirteen of them," she said. "The vet says it's unbelievable that all of them are alive and healthy."

What an opportunity I had missed! It was I, not the children, who needed the lesson on prayer. If I had asked about the puppies the following Sunday, we all would have been blessed by the Lord's answer. Fear and unbelief had held me back.

Does God always say "Yes" to our prayers? What if one or more of the puppies had died? That would have been another missed opportunity, a chance to teach that God always wants what is best for us. I could have said that we can continue to trust God and his love for us even when he sometimes says "No." The children might have handled such an outcome better than I would have thought possible.

A pastor friend told me that when he visits a home where there is illness, if there is a small child in the family, he asks that child to join him in prayer for the need. He is convinced that the believing prayers of little children carry great weight with the heavenly Father.

I'm not the only adult who needs to listen to what children can teach us about prayer. An all-night prayer meeting was in progress in Jerusalem. This was a crisis time for the infant Christian church. Herod had arrested James and beheaded him. Next on his hit list was Peter. In the maximum security prison, Peter slept. In the home of Mary and her son, John Mark, the Christians prayed. Rumor had it that Herod would order Peter's execution the following day.

That night God intervened directly and miraculously. Guards slept. Chains fell away from Peter. Iron gates opened without a squeak. Peter was free! An angel guided him away from the prison.

Mary's home must have been known as a gathering place for praying people. Peter knew exactly where to go. He knocked on the outer door and called for someone to open it. Rhoda, a young girl, responded to the knock. Without opening the door, she recognized Peter's voice. She ran into the middle of the pray-ers to tell them that their answer was at the door.

"You're crazy!" they told her. But Rhoda insisted. Peter was the one for whom they had been praying, and Peter stood at the door.

"Then it must be his angel," they reasoned. Finally someone opened the door. There stood Peter. Only a young girl, Rhoda, had faith to believe that the Lord had done the impossible (Acts 12:1-17).

Often the spontaneous prayers of children serve as a reproof to our own hesitancy and delay. Prayer is here-and-now communication with God. "Pray without ceasing" (1 Thessalonians 5:17).

A mother brought her two daughters and foster son to register them for our community vacation Bible school. The leader asked the mother not to register the foster child. People in our small community knew that the boy had been born to a woman infected with the AIDS virus. The leader reasoned that at least one family would withdraw its children if this child attended.

On the way home, the four-year-old boy was crying because he had not been allowed to stay at the school. His mother was also crying.

"Are you angry, Mommy?"

"No, I'm just sad."

"Is he a bad man?"

"No, he's not bad. We just need to pray for him."

The child needed no further urging. Immediately he prayed, "Dear Jesus, please make that man let me go to Bible school."

That evening the leader called the mother and said that her son was welcome to attend. He had discovered that the class's teacher was a qualified respite care person for HIV children. An assistant teacher in the class could take over if any special care were required.

Simplicity. Spontaneity. Expectation. These terms describe childlike prayer.

To Be Childlike

1. How can you approach prayer with childlike simplicity? Can you capture some of Ollie's spontaneity? "All us kids love ya."

2. When opportunity is given, will you pray aloud in a group? Avoid pious clichés implying that prayer is a foreign language which only an in-group can speak. Develop a simple conversational style that encourages others also to pray aloud.

3. Can you trust God with occasional doubts and anger? He is big enough to handle our fears and frustrations. He knows about them even if we deny them.

4. Do you limit prayer to intercession and overlook the centrality of prayer, the relationship of love, and worship of our Lord? Jesus instructed us to pray, "Thy name be hallowed! Thy kingdom come! Thy will be done" in me!

5. What message from your Bible reading has been the Lord's voice to you this week? Record it in your journal. Is your Bible reading an exercise in prayerful listening?

6. Have your heard the Lord speak in nature, in bird songs, in rain slamming against the window? Have you heard him speak through the voice of a friend, or in a written word? How much of your prayer is listening?

Humility and Dependence

THE preschool teacher at our church school was telling the story of Zacchaeus to three-year-olds.

"What if Jesus came to your house today," proposed the teacher. "Would you ask Jesus to come in? Would you want Jesus to stay at your house?"

The children responded eagerly. How exciting to have Jesus come to our house! All except Peter. He said, "No!" Emphatically!

The teacher did not probe Peter's refusal, and tried to continue with the story. But Peter would not be ignored. "Do you know why I wouldn't want Jesus to come to my house? 'Cause my room is a mess!"

How did the teacher conclude that lesson? I want to think that it went like this: "If Jesus came to your house, Peter, I hope you would say to him, 'I'm sorry my room is a mess, Jesus.' I think Jesus would take your hand and say, 'Come, Peter, let's clean it up.' Then together you and Jesus would pick up your toys, and hang up your clothes, and make your room clean and tidy."

I'm thankful that I invited the Lord Jesus into my life before I fully grasped the mess in my own room: unresolved fears, guilts real and imagined. The Lord has taken my hand. Little by little, as I have been able to handle it, he has led me into dark and cluttered corners. We're still working at cleaning up my room.

"Who is the greatest in the kingdom of heaven?" the followers of Jesus asked.

In reply, Jesus used an object lesson. He called a child to stand among them. He said, "Truly I tell you, unless you change and become like children, you will never enter the kingdom of heaven. Whoever becomes humble like this child is the greatest in the kingdom of heaven" (Matt. 18:1-10).

Jesus erected a signpost on the road to childlikeness: *Humility! A humble spirit!*

Richard Foster in *Celebration of Discipline* comments, "Wherever there is trouble over who is the greatest, there is trouble over who is the least. That is the crux of the matter for us, isn't it? Most of us know we will never be the greatest; just don't let us be the least."[1]

Never will I learn childlike humility by comparing myself with the citizens of the world; not even by comparing myself with other church members. I am likely to search out the person limping along in the Christian walk. Then I console myself that at least I'm doing better than that one.

In a parable Jesus told, the Pharisee prayed, "Thank you, Lord, that I'm so much better than these other people" (paraphrased).

The publican prayed, "God, be merciful to me, a sinner."

Jesus ended that parable, "for all who exalt themselves will be humbled, but all who humble themselves will be exalted" (Luke 18:9-14).

I think it is no coincidence that people who heard this parable immediately brought their children to Jesus, asking him to touch them.

"Let the little children come to me," he said, "and do not stop them; for it is to such as these that the kingdom of God belongs. Truly I tell you, whoever does not receive the kingdom of God as a little child will never enter it" (Luke 18:15-17).

We do not easily learn humility. Neither did Jesus' disciples. All through his life with them, Jesus taught by his words and by his example.

In the solemn gathering before the crucifixion, Jesus gave a powerful object lesson in humility. He was well aware that the Father had entrusted everything to him, and that he had come from God and was going back to God. Knowing all this, Jesus knelt down before his confused disciples and washed their dirty feet.

"Do you know what I have done to you?" Jesus asked "You call me Teacher and Lord—and you are right, for that is what I am. So if I, your Lord and Teacher, have washed your feet, you also ought to wash one another's feet" (John 13:3-17).

In *The Company of the Committed*, Elton Trueblood says of this incident,

> We need to contemplate the present applicability of an act which combines humility and loving service, which renounces unequivocally all struggles for prestige and preeminence, and which indicates the radical nature of the break that must be exhibited between the standards of the church and the standards of the world.[2]

True childlike humility develops as I comprehend more of the infinite greatness of the Lord. As I mature spiritually and know the Lord more intimately, I become more keenly aware of the finite smallness of me, his child. That is fertile ground for the growth of a healthy humility. This infinite, great, powerful, all-knowing God loves little me!

We were guests at a four-generation family Thanksgiving dinner. After the meal, each person in turn stated one reason for thankfulness in life. Little Hannah sat nestled on her father's lap. When father's turn came, he hesitated for a moment. Hannah helped him out. "I know what, Daddy. You're thankful for me!"

Was that lack of humility on Hannah's part? No, only the honest acceptance of who she was in relation to her loving parents. I express humility when I become a consenting child of God.

I am aware that false humility has kept me from inviting friends to my home. Or was it undue pride? The house wasn't clean enough. I didn't have time to prepare a fancy meal. My husband with his outgoing warmth helped me to see my own mess in this respect.

We were preparing to move into an old house we had bought. We left our apartment one morning for a day of work at the house. I took enough food for a fast lunch. We had hired a neighborhood man to clean the basement for us, and he was there that day.

As I was preparing our four hot dogs, I was appalled to hear my husband invite the man to share our lunch. The fourth hot dog was divided between the two men. By then we had established a closer relationship with a new neighbor.

When we show childlike humility, we sometimes allow the Lord to show us that his plans for us are far greater than we have dared to dream.

Naomi, age two, was in the bakery shop with her parents. As they waited, Naomi's father pointed to a penny on the floor. Naomi was delighted with the find.

The customer ahead of them, seeing the child's joy in finding a penny, held out to her the handful of change he had just received. Naomi looked puzzled, then somberly placed her penny in his outstretched hand. The hurt look changed to wonder as he poured all the coins into her hand!

Sometimes I misunderstand the intentions of others and of the Lord. That's when the Lord loves to surprise me. I may misinterpret, believing that he is asking for my puny little penny. But he is holding out his hands full of treasures to me.

Naomi was five when her family was living about a hundred miles from her grandparents. Her father was nearing the end of his medical residency. Lois, her mother, knew that they would soon be moving across several states. So she took the children to see their grandparents as often as possible. Naomi, oldest of the three, loved those visits.

One day Lois proposed, "Naomi, would you like to be with Grandma and Grandpa all by yourself for a couple of days, just you, without Christine and Jonathan?"

Naomi's response was emphatic and negative. Several days later Lois asked again and got the same response.

"I thought you would like being with Grandma and Grandpa and have them all to yourself."

"Mommy, I can't drive the car! And I don't know the way to Grandma's house all by myself!"

No doubt Naomi made a realistic evaluation of her own capability, a humble, self-knowing one. But she had failed to understand that her mother meant she would take her to her grandparents' home, and bring her home.

This reminds me again that when I am as humble as a little child, the Lord loves to surprise me. And when I admit to myself and to him that I'm not sure of my way, my heavenly Parent is ready to guide.

Naomi had a satisfying visit alone with Grandma and Grandpa.

J. B. Phillips in *God Our Contemporary* comments,

> Christ says in effect, if men are to grasp the purpose of God, they must begin again to learn as children. . . . Surely the force of his remarks is that there must be a return to humility in the God-man relationship before human knowledge and the acquisition of truth have any real meaning. . . . Jesus is concerned to establish the fact that compared with the immensely complex wisdom of God, we are children, and that until we accept that fact with humility, our knowledge will either be a burden to us or may lead us further and further from essential truth."[3]

Foster states it succinctly: "Study demands humility. . . . Arrogance and a teachable spirit are mutually exclusive. . . . Not only is study directly dependent upon humility, but it is conducive to it."[4]

As we study and increase in wisdom, we may be tempted to believe that now we can move beyond humility. Unwittingly, we may develop a haughty spirit which is the opposite of a humble one.

Young king Solomon prayed with humility: "O Lord, my God, you have made your servant king in place of my father David, although I am only a little child; I do not know how to go out or come in. . . . Give your servant therefore an understanding mind to govern your people, able to discern between good and evil" (1 Kings 3:3-10). But his life story reveals that he grew to glory in his own power, wealth, wisdom, and pleasures. Solomon moved far away from a childlike spirit.

In my class of nine-to-eleven-year-olds, we were studying about Christian family living. Each child made a take-home chart. Across the top they wrote the names of the people in their household. Down the left side, they listed the days of the week. They were to fill in the blanks each day, telling of one kind and loving thing they had done for each person in addition to usual household chores.

Judy returned with a completed chart next Sunday. On several days for both big brother and grandpa, she had written, "I stayed out of his way." That is loving humility!

As I progress in humility before the Lord, I learn that he is dependable. I am free to express fears, doubts, and find his comforting reassurance.

One day at the dinner table, Tiffany burst into tears. "What is wrong?" her parents asked. Tiffany related that parents of a classmate had separated. "I don't know which one of you I would want to live with," she sobbed. "'Cause I love you both so much." Her parents assured her that was a decision she would never have to make.

Humility before God opens the way for our heavenly Parent to reassure us. He will never leave us. He will never forsake.

Who is the Christian I know who best exemplifies childlike humility? I contacted that person and asked for permission to use his name. I am not surprised that he chose to remain anonymous. He had retired from a position with a large mission organization. Though past age seventy, he was still in demand as a consultant for missionary enterprises around the world.

His childlikeness glowed in his face, unaffected, joyous, charming. When he prayed, it seemed to me that his slight stature touched heaven. He prayed as a child, aware of his need to grow. Yet he was confident of God's love for him right now, not because of any merit of his own, but because of who God is.

Whenever this man taught an elective church school class, I enrolled. I sensed his ability to raise us all to a common place where we stood before God.

One frequent class member had cerebral palsy. A brilliant seminary student, he was preparing for a Christian writing career. He made excellent contributions to class discussion even though he struggled painfully to enunciate words. In earlier classes, I had seen other leaders interrupt him and presume to finish his statements for him. This teacher waited and listened. Often he repeated and enlarged on the young man's statement to be sure the whole class understood.

Another regular in this man's classes was an elderly woman from the government housing project, unusual in that affluent church. She always sat in the front row and took part in discussion. Sometimes her comments seemed to have no relevance to our subject. Graciously this teacher seemed to find some grain of truth in what she said and lifted it up to enhance the lesson.

That man humbled himself, not by putting himself down, but by lifting up every other person to the level where he stood. We received the message that each of us is counted among the children of one heavenly Father; each one is loved and precious just as we are.

Childlike humility helps me to relate rightly to God. He is Creator and Redeemer. I am creature and mortal. I am a redeemed one. I know I can depend on him.

My relationship of childlike humility with Parent-God opens the way to a Christian balance of dependence with others. I see that before the Lord, we are all on the same level. We need to hold hands with each other, give mutual support, and be supported by each other.

When I depend on others, I make myself vulnerable. I have depended on some Christian friends who betrayed my trust. Living by Jesus' standards does involve risk.

There is a self that makes me want to set myself above others and puff myself up as someone great. That self is as nauseating as the one that puts myself down, constantly telling others how worthless I am.

A patronizing attitude demands that others always depend on me. A childish dependence demands that others always be available to me. Somewhere between these two, and founded firmly on our dependence upon the Lord, is the interdependence that should characterize the Christian family unit and the extended family of God.

The apostle Peter wrote to his Christian friends, "All of you must clothe yourselves with humility in your dealings with one another" (1 Pet. 5:5).

A cartoon, author anonymous, showed a person in underwear and the comment, "Many of us would be scantily clad if clothed only in our humility."

To Be Childlike

1. "I am convinced that God loves me, not because of who I am, but because of who he is." Can you write that sentence in your journal and sign your name to it?

2. What in your life is still "in a mess"? Can you take the hand which Jesus holds out to you to work with him at cleaning up the mess?

3. What treasures is the Lord holding out to you? Are you ready to open your hand and receive them?

4. Do you have an acquaintance that you consider to be beneath you? It will show in your words and actions, even if you think you are hiding it. What can you plan to do with that person to impress upon yourself that we stand equal before God?

5. Humility is your self in relation with God, with yourself, and with others. Humiliation is what we do to each other or receive from others in put-downs.

Are you guilty of humiliating others? Your spouse, children, others close to you?

6. Are you sensitive to the significance of dependable Christian friends? How do you show appreciation to them?

7. On whom do you depend? Who depends on you? For what? Is there a mutual interdependence which exemplifies Christian humility, or a childish dependence, or an attempt to run others' lives?

8. Meditate on the Beatitudes. Matthew 5:3-11. Do they describe the childlike qualities that we are seeking to develop?

Sense of Awe
and Wonder

O N Easter Sunday morning, we attended a large church, perhaps 1,500 in the congregation. An organ and an orchestra accompanied two choirs. They sang a magnificent anthem of praise, ending in a great crescendo of alleluias.

The audience sat in hushed reverence. Then a small child's voice, audible throughout the sanctuary, exclaimed, "WOW!"

The smiling pastor commented, "Thank you. I think he spoke for all of us."

Ravi Zacharias, worldwide Bible teacher, said in a radio message that the older we get, the more it takes to fill our hearts with wonder.

Wonder. Curiosity. Awe. These words describe something of the childlike spirit that Jesus commended. How often we allow pride to obscure the wonder.

Pride came close to condemning a man to the living death of leprosy. An Israelite child, slave to Naaman's wife, opened the way for his healing.

Raiding soldiers from the country of Aram (Syria) had snatched the girl from her home and sold her into slavery. That child carried within her, into a foreign land, a sanctified faith-imagination in the greatness and power of the God of Elisha.

"If only my master could meet the prophet who lives in Samaria, he would cure him of his leprosy." How could this child, so sinned against, show compassion to her captors? Compassion is another quality of childlikeness. We will speak more of that later.

The message was relayed to Naaman, and by Naaman to his superior, the king of Aram. It became a matter of diplomatic import between two countries not on peaceful terms with each other.

With a supply of kingly gifts, Naaman and his entourage set off for Samaria. They sought an audience with Israel's king and handed him a letter from the king of Aram.

"This is to inform you that I am sending to you my servant Naaman. I beg you to rid him of his disease."

King Ahab called an emergency cabinet meeting. "He is doing this just to pick a quarrel with us. He is trumping up some excuse to attack us again. Am I God, to kill or make alive?"

The news leaked out. Elisha heard and sent a message to the king. "Let the man come to me, and he shall know that there is a prophet in Israel."

Naaman eventually reached Elisha's home. A servant met him and reported, "My master Elisha says, if you will go and wash seven times in the Jordan, your flesh will be restored, and you will be clean."

Naaman was furious! He had his standards, and they were not being met. He expected Elisha to come out and greet him, but he met only Elisha's servant. He expected Elisha to invoke the Lord his God by name. There was no mention of the Lord God in Elisha's message. He expected the prophet to wave his hand over the leprosy sores.

Elisha and his God had not responded to Naaman's expectations of how a visiting dignitary should be treated. He stalked off in a haughty rage. He was commander of the armies of Aram! God or at least God's prophet should have given him an audience more deserving of his position. The rivers of Aram were far superior to this muddy little Jordan creek!

Had it not been for Naaman's servants, he would have returned home with all his pride and outraged dignity, and with his leprosy.

Naaman listened to his servants and agreed to take the seven dips into Jordan's waters. "He went down and immersed himself seven times in the Jordan, according to the word of the man of God; his flesh was restored like the flesh of a young boy, and he was clean."

Surely it was not by chance that the Bible records that his flesh was as a child's. Naaman had to lay aside his pride in himself, his position, his place of dwelling, and enter into wholeness through the gate of childlikeness (2 Kings 5, paraphrased, summarized).

What about the child who initiated the healing for Naaman? Did Elisha have a reputation for healing lepers? No. Jesus said, "There were also many lepers in Israel in the time of the prophet Elisha, and none of them was cleansed except Naaman the Syrian" (Luke 4:27).

Perhaps the child had heard of other miracles that Elisha had performed. All we know is that she had a sense of awe and wonder in the greatness of Elisha's God. Her faith seemed to center, not in past experience, but in the reality of who God is. She felt compassion even for her captors, and for Naaman, an enemy to her own people.

What a contrast between this slave child of the Old Testament and the people of Nazareth! They were honored with Jesus as their synagogue speaker. Yet they perceived Jesus only as the hometown man, so much a part of only the physical world. They had no awe and wonder. Instead, they were filled with rage that led to them driving Jesus out of the synagogue and out of their town (Luke 4:27-30).

Jesus sought constantly to open the eyes and minds of his listeners to the wonders of the world God created for us. Jesus sought to help them grasp the symbolism, the relationship to the reign of God that he was proclaiming.

Look at the birds in the air, look in wonder. They don't sow or reap or gather into barns.

Look at the lilies of the fields, look in wonder. They

don't spin their own clothes.

Look at the hair on your head, look in wonder. Your Creator has counted those hairs!

Look about you, look in wonder, says Jesus. Do the heavens declare God's glory to you? Does the Creation help you grasp the greatness of God? As a radio speaker said, the kingdom of God is an education in wonderment.

Jesse was supposedly getting ready for school, second grade. His mother became impatient as she heard him and his friend in conversation in his room. As she approached the room, she saw that together they were paging through an insect book.

"Oh, wow! Cicadas! I love them."

"Luna moths! Awesome!"

Mother decided to give them five more minutes to marvel at these "common bugs" that she never thought twice about.

I was preparing to take part in our Bible study group, working with the assigned passage, Matthew 6. I meditated as I took a walk along the country road near our home.

Soon I became aware that clumps of day lilies and Queen Anne's lace bloomed in profusion along the roadside. Was Jesus looking at a similar roadside scene when he pointed out something to his followers? "Look at the lilies of the field, here for a day and gone tomorrow. Yet even King Solomon in all his glory could not compare with these flowers" (paraphrased).

The brilliant orange blossoms of day lilies open at

daybreak and fade by evening. The delicate Queen Anne's lace is named for royalty. That evening, a bowl of day lilies and Queen Anne's lace graced the table at the center of our Bible study group.

When parents brought young children to Jesus, the disciples tried to send them away. This aroused Jesus to indignation. "Let the little children come to me; do not stop them; for it is to such as these that the kingdom of God belongs. . . . Whoever does not receive the kingdom of God as a little child will never enter it" (Mark 10:13-16).

In his book *Reaching*, Morton Kelsey says,

> What is the quality of children that opens them to the kingdom? Is it not their wonder about the world; their openness to the spiritual dimension as well as the physical, and their constantly seeking, searching to know both the physical world around them and the spiritual one?. . . One of the reasons so few of us ever come to our full stature as human beings is that we have lost this spirit of childlike seeking, something that is very difficult to regain once it has been conditioned out of us."[1]

A great-grandfather told me, after a visit with his three-year-old great-granddaughter, "Most of her sentences begin with 'Why?' or 'Maybe.' " A spirit of wonder and a creative mind let her imagine the "maybe" to her own questions.

I was driving guests with several small children through state forest lands to a mountain lookout near our home. I was probably thinking about what I would serve them for lunch. A six-year-old boy broke through my preoccupation.

"There's millions and millions of people in the world, and they haven't seen these trees. Do you think that there is a tree that nobody has ever seen? Maybe it's a tree standing by itself, and there isn't even another tree near it."

Aristotle is quoted as saying that philosophy begins in wonder.

Do I let my preoccupation crowd out my capacity to wonder? Am I too busy to see the trees, the wonders of God's Creation? Do I see beyond them, to the wonders of the world of the spirit?

Two small children were on their way to church with their grandparents. It was raining.

"Where does the rain come from?" asked the tiny girl.

"God sends the rain," said Grandmother.

Her older brother needed to show off his superior knowledge. "The rain comes from the clouds, doesn't it?"

"Yes, but God made the clouds," explained Grandmother.

It was a new insight for the boy. In wonder he asked, "Does God get his hands wet?"

The childlike Christian sees God constantly getting his hands wet as he handles the affairs of the universe he created.

The childlike Christian also seeks to nurture the

sense of awe and wonder as it relates to the spiritual, the kingdom within. Jesus said, "I thank you, Father, Lord of heaven and earth, because you have hidden these things from the wise and intelligent and have revealed them to infants; yes, Father, for such was your gracious will" (Matt. 11:25-26).

Jesus prayed that prayer while being doubted, scorned, and rejected by people who had lost their sense of wonder and awe, even in the face of his miracles.

Imprisoned John the Baptist had yielded to doubt and sent friends to ask Jesus, "Are you the one who is to come, or should we expect someone else?"

"Go and tell John what you hear and see; the blind receive their sight, the lame walk, the lepers are cleansed, the deaf hear, the dead are raised, and the poor have good news brought to them."

Jesus went on to denounce the towns that had seen these miracles and responded with apathy. Alas for Chorazin, Bethsaida, and Capernaum! People of Tyre and Sidon would have responded with awe and wonder leading to repentance. Even Sodom, if it had witnessed the works of Jesus, would have saved itself from destruction.

"At that time," we are told, Jesus thanked the Father that the spiritual realities hidden from the learned and intelligent ones were revealed to the simple ones, the childlike (Matt. 11).

The book, *Children in Community*, tells how one community of Christians educates its children. The

Bruderhof Communities seek to preserve those child-like qualities so precious in the eyes of the Lord.

The introduction to this delightful book states, "We confess and witness that to open our hearts to a child is to listen to a language that comes from the heart of God." I quote a poem by Jane Clement, one of their teachers.

> Child, though I take your hand
> and walk in the snow;
> though we follow the track of the mouse together,
> though we try to unlock together the mystery
> of the printed word, and slowly discover
> why two and three make five
> always in an uncertain world—
> child, though I am meant to teach you much,
> what is it, in the end,
> except that together we are
> meant to be children of the same Father
> and I must unlearn
> all the adult structure
> and the encumbering years
> and you must teach me
> to look at the earth and the heaven
> with your fresh wonder.[2]

To Be Childlike

1. Read some of the psalms that express the author's wonder at God's world, God expressing himself in Creation. Suggestions: Psalms 19, 29, 65, 104, 147, 148.

2. Look to find God involved in the affairs of your own life, the microscopic view. Look to see him in the affairs of the whole world and of the universe, the telescopic view.

3. Wonder is one of the primary elements of worship. How can you prepare yourself for childlike wonder (WOW!) at the next worship service you attend?

4. Try some exercises in faith-imagination:

• You are alone with Jesus in a boat on the Sea of Galilee. What do you want to tell him? What does he say to you?

• You take a walk with Jesus to some place that holds happy memories for you.

• You go with Jesus to some spot where you have experienced deep hurts.

• You are alone. Place an empty chair before you, and visualize Jesus seated on that chair. What will you say to each other?

6

Simplicity

DO you remember the fairy tale about the emperor's new clothes? Two men convinced the emperor that they could weave cloth and make a suit of clothes for him that would have magical powers. The cloth would be visible only to those worthy of their position. To those unworthy of their positions, the cloth would be invisible.

The emperor visited the weavers, busy at their looms. He gave no hint that he couldn't see any cloth. The men cut and stitched and fitted the new garments, but still the emperor saw nothing. The men proclaimed their job completed. The king's courtiers stood around, exclaiming in delight at the elegance of the emperor's new clothes.

How could the emperor admit to his courtiers that he saw no clothes, and so confess that he was not worthy to be emperor? Of course the courtiers couldn't see any clothes, either. But if they said so, they would discredit themselves before their emperor and their peers.

So the emperor appeared before his adoring populace in his magical new clothes. It took the cry of a little child to save them all from their foolishness. "The emperor is naked! He isn't wearing any clothes!"

Only the unsophisticated child, in honest simplicity, dared to voice the obvious. He had no need to fear questioning or proving his station in life. In a children's drama production of this parable, the emperor appeared in long underwear, and the audience still got the message.

In their simplicity, children may be more perceptive than we are in seeing among their acquaintances people who speak and act as Jesus did.

I was blessed with a husband who reminded children of Jesus. He wore a beard long before beards became commonplace. On vacation, we visited a large church. In the fellowship hall after the worship service, a small boy approached him and said shyly, "Hello, Jesus."

In our living room hangs a copy of the painting of *Hands*, by J. Reed. The hands extend from white-robed arms and rest on white-robed knees. One hand is cupped upward in a gesture of receiving, and the other extends outward in a gesture of giving.

One neighborhood child, to whom we were acting grandparents, gazed long at the painting. Then he said, "That's Granddad's hands, isn't it?"

Charles Dickens has been quoted as saying, "I love these little people. And it is not a slight thing when they, who are so fresh from God, love us."

My niece Lois was two years old when my mother died. A few days later, Lois was at my home. As I took her to the bathroom, we passed Grandma's bedroom.

"Grandma doesn't sleep here anymore," she told me. "She sleeps in Jesus' house now."

Her simple perception of death eased my own grieving.

Several years ago I read a cartoon which portrayed that same simplicity. The boy, romping in the park, heard a woman talking with his mother and saying that she had lost her dad.

The boy came to the woman and asked, "Can I help you look? How come we're not looking for him? We can help you look."

The woman tried to explain that she had not lost her dad there in the park. The child's mother whispered to him.

He turned to the woman. "You didn't lose your dad. God took him. When God takes somebody, they're okay 'cause they're with God. Do you understand?"

"I do now," agreed the woman.

Robbie Trent in *Your Child and God* tells of a child

who walked with his mother to the top of a hill and stood there looking at a crimson sunset. Suddenly he held his mother's hand a bit tighter. "Mother," he said, "I want to pray." Before she could answer, he bowed his head and said softly, "One, two, three, four, five, six, seven, eight, nine, ten." He had just learned to count. And who shall say that the understanding Father heart of God failed to receive that offering of praise and gratitude?[1]

I relish the simplicity of the boy who heard that Jesus was concerned about the lack of food. He offered his little picnic lunch of five barley loaves and two small fish. The disciples saw only the incongruity of the offering in the face of the need, more than five thousand hungry people. In the hands of Jesus, the boy's lunch fed everyone and filled twelve baskets of leftovers.

One aspect of the simplicity of children is expressed in their sense of expectation, the "todayness" of everything.

The year was 1969. My niece Marilynn, her husband, and two small daughters were in Saigon, Vietnam. Conscientious objectors to the war in progress, they had volunteered to work under Vietnam Christian Service.

Marilynn, a physician, was on duty in an orphanage where she saw a baby boy, perhaps four weeks old. She knew that with their limited staff and the scarcity of food, he had little chance for survival. They took the baby home and started adoption proceedings under Vietnamese law.

Then came the Tet offensive, with Saigon under attack. American families with children were advised to leave. But little John's adoption proceedings were hopelessly entangled in crippled government bureau-cracy. Another couple with a small child, also under Vietnam Christian Service, left Saigon and took Marilynn's two daughters with them.

The children came to live with Grandma and Grandpa to await their parents and John. Kerry, age six, had some concept of distance and time, and the uncertainties that had shadowed their last weeks in Saigon.

Cheryl, age four, lived in happy expectation. Every morning she awoke in hope. "Maybe today my mommy and daddy and John will come."

That simplicity of expectation never faded through the three long months that we waited for them to clear John's adoption. Only then could they bring the boy out of Vietnam and to America. Cheryl's expec-tation was new every morning.

My usual place for morning devotional time is by a window that faces east. Often high clouds catch the glow of approaching sunrise long before the sun tops the tree line. The spectacle of the glowing clouds stirs the prayer of my heart. "Maybe today you will return, Lord Jesus. Maybe these are the glorious clouds that herald your coming."

Sometimes children express the simplicity of their spiritual awareness by actions rather than words. In the Advent season, the children in my church school class of nine-to-eleven-year-olds were making simple nativity figures. They were just using construction paper cones with Styrofoam ball heads. As they worked each week, we read and talked about the birth of Jesus.

Each week they took home a completed figure. I encouraged them to set up their own nativity scene at home. On the last Sunday, they made the figure for the baby Jesus. His body was a small white cone with blue bands for swaddling, his manger a bed of shredded yellow construction paper.

At a church meeting the following week, one mother spoke to me.

"I know my son can give you a hard time. And maybe you think that he doesn't hear and doesn't learn anything. But I must tell you what happened in my son's room when he brought home his baby Jesus last week.

"When I went into his room, I found that he had completely cleared the top of his dresser. The only things on it were his nativity figures.

"You must understand what the top of his dresser usually looks like. It's the place for his treasures. You know—baseball cards, rocks, bottle caps, dinosaur models, a horseshoe. It's the one place in his room that I may never, never touch. Now only the nativity figures were there."

If the nativity figures had found a place among his other treasures, I would have been gratified. But when he gave the center to the Lord Jesus, he had no place for anything else to be considered a treasure.

That boy's actions became for me a parable illustrating Jesus' words: "The kingdom of heaven is like a merchant in search of fine pearls; on finding one pearl of great value, he went and sold all that he had and bought it" (Matt. 13:45-46).

When we become as little children, we open ourselves to the capacity to be simple, spontaneous, aware, and open to life.

What is simplicity? In *The Notebook on Spiritual Discipline*, Maxie Dunham calls it "uncomplicated expectation." He comments on the healing of the lame man at the temple gate in Acts 3.

> There is an exciting and challenging message in this healing experience. The early Christians lived daily in expectation of miracles. They believed that what Christ had promised, he would perform. Their faith was powerful because it was so genuine, so deep and uncomplicated that it enabled them to transcend themselves and be free channels of Christ's unchecked, undiluted grace and power.[2]

Jesse's mother gave birth to her second child on December 29. During Advent, Jesse, not quite three years old, was hearing stories about the birth of Jesus. Along with anticipating Christmas, he was also looking for the birth of their baby.

At a prenatal visit with his mother, the doctor asked Jesse, "So, what kind of baby do you think this is going to be?"

Without hesitation, Jesse said, "I think it's going to be baby Jesus." For Jesse, the birth of Jesus was just as "here and now" as the birth of his baby sister.

Children experience the simplicity of their spiritual world, the "today-ness" that says, the kingdom of God is within me, and among us. It is not just something that happened two thousand years ago, not something only in the dim and distant future when I go to heaven. It is today.

Naomi's mother found a paper among things she had brought home from summer camp. Across the top was printed, JESUS IS THE ANSWER. The instructions were to write two questions you would like to ask Jesus.

Naomi had written,

1. Why did you let Pilate kill you?
2. May I have ten people at my birthday party?

The child saw no incongruity between the deepest theological mysteries and the concern for her birthday party next month.

I was a cabin counselor at a summer camp for children from an inner-city mission. As we gathered for a campfire time, Jim came swinging a big stick. It came threateningly close to some children's heads. I took the stick and promised to return it when the campfire ended.

Jim responded to the message that evening and went off with his counselor for a quiet talk. I was still seated by the fire when he returned. I handed his stick to him.

"I don't need it now," Jim said. He broke it in two, threw it into the embers, and walked away.

Then Roscoe came to the fireside. "Aw, who burned that good stick?" he asked. I told him that Jim had decided he did not need it and had thrown it in the fire.

"But it was my stick," protested Roscoe. "He took it from me."

I tried to explain that Jim had an encounter with Jesus that evening. Now he felt he didn't need a big stick to scare other kids any more.

There was silence. Then Roscoe whispered, "I met Jesus tonight, too. I'm sort of glad Jim threw the stick in the fire 'cause I guess I don't need it anymore, either." He kicked at the embers and walked away.

I heard a Christian minister tell how he was approached by a friend with the question, "Do you believe God's Word?"

"Of course," responded the minister.

Then the friend asked, "What part of it did you believe for today?"

Childlike simplicity lets me believe God's Word as it applies to my life for today, planning my birthday party, or disposing of the big stick I may be carrying around. Childlike simplicity lets me view the present moment in the light of God's presence in my life.

To Be Childlike

1. What have you been withholding from the Lord's service because you didn't think it was good enough? A phone call to a lonely neighbor? A letter to a shut-in? Your comments in the Bible study group, withheld because you perceive others as better educated? Remember what Jesus did with five loaves and two small fish.

2. Do you search to see the Lord Jesus in the faces of Christian family and friends? Do you look for something Christlike rather than looking for faults?

3. Are you carrying around any big sticks that you need to throw into the fire?

4. Do you read God's Word, searching for his message to you for today?

5. Do you "feel" as well as "think" into Bible stories, to identify with people, situations, and the present-day Lord?

6. What material possessions get in the way of childlike simplicity in your life? Have you cleared off the clutter of things, of emotions, from your dresser, so that Jesus may reign as the supreme treasure of your life?

7

Desire to Grow

ON his third birthday, Jesse sat on his mother's lap as she read one of his favorite books. Then he sat turning the pages, looking at the pictures. At one page he paused, looked and looked, then said wistfully, "I wish I could read those words!"

The little child knows that he doesn't know. As I seek to become childlike, I must recognize that all through my earthly life, I shall be only a beginner. I want to develop that desire to grow, especially to keep growing in the spiritual life, the life of God's kingdom.

A person confident of knowing it all may face a boring future, and may also be a bore to others. An acquaintance, head of his department at college, wrote a book in his area of expertise. The book was published and was widely accepted as a textbook at colleges and universities across the country. He confessed to a deep depression because he felt he had achieved all of his life's goals and had nothing more to live for.

If we ever reach such a point in our spiritual lives,

we have lost the aim to become childlike.

In his book on *Contemplative Prayer*, Thomas Merton says,

> One cannot begin to face the real difficulties of the life of prayer and meditation unless one is first perfectly content to be a beginner and really experience himself as one who knows little or nothing, and has a desperate need to learn the bare rudiments. Those who think they "know" from the beginning will never, in fact, come to know anything. We do not want to be beginners. But let us be convinced of the fact that we will never be anything else but beginners, all our life!"[1]

When I approach the Lord in a childlike spirit, I believe he will pave the way for me to desire to grow. That means more than just loading me with facts. It means helping me to grow into being, not just learning.

Once I prayed my usual Sunday morning prayer, that the Lord would help me be a good teacher to the children in my class. My devotional reading was Matthew 18. Again I heard the words of the Master Teacher: "Unless you change and become like children, you will never enter the kingdom of heaven. Whoever becomes humble like this child is the greatest in the kingdom of heaven. Whoever welcomes one such child in my name welcomes me."

I changed my prayer to fit this text: "Lord, help me to become a good learner."

My first lesson came during the worship service.

One of the children I picked up at a foster home and brought to church was five-year-old Jayson. He was usually the most restless one during the worship service. I had repeatedly asked him to sit quietly during the times of prayer and Bible reading and not to ask me for things.

I explained that when we pray, we are talking with God. When the Bible is read, we are listening to God talking to us. I expected him to be quiet during those times. That way, he would not disturb me and other people who were having conversations with God.

That morning, Jayson sat motionless during prayer time. After the "Amen," I whispered to him my appreciation that he was quiet while I prayed. He looked up at me and said, "Well, I was praying too."

During the church school hour, I faced a class of six-to-eight-year-olds, a younger age than I usually taught. Was I teaching at a level that reached them?

The Lord showed me that my expectations were far too low. The lesson centered on the concept of new life, the eternal life that God gives.

Tracy told us about her little sister's heart deformity, that she had a hole in her heart. Are lots of babies born with holes in their hearts? the children asked. Melissa needed to talk about a baby brother who had died at birth. Melissa herself was an adopted child, another topic that aroused comment. One child talked about a schoolmate who had been killed in an automobile accident that year.

I was astonished to hear that these children were

expressing desire to grow in the greatest spiritual issues of life and suffering and death. I know that today I am still a beginner.

In *Celebration of Discipline*, Richard Foster writes, "Like a child taking first steps, we are learning through success and failure, confident that we have a present Teacher who through the Holy Spirit will guide us into all truth."[2]

Will growth end when earthly life ends? I believe that desire to grow and opportunities for growth will continue through all eternity.

A child expresses excitement about physical growth when a parent makes a birthday mark of growth on the closet door. It's exciting to know that one is growing taller, exciting to put on last winter's clothes and discover they are now too small. I want to maintain an excitement about continuing to grow.

Sophia was learning to jump rope. She caught on quickly. She liked to have mother nearby to count how many jumps until she missed.

"Sophia, you jumped twenty-five times!" said mother. Sophia threw back her head and laughed with pure joy over her accomplishment. She laughed and laughed. It was contagious. Soon mother was laughing, also.

The body of a healthy child grows naturally in response to good nutrition and exercise. I want to nourish my spiritual life with regular feeding on God's word and regular exercising in obedience to his commands.

The prophet Jeremiah put himself in a position where God could commission him and use him. He confessed, "Ah, Lord God! Truly I do not know how to speak, for I am only a boy." In that childlike spirit, Jeremiah became God's spokesperson (Jer. 1:4-8).

Michael Quoist thinks it is disastrous when grown-ups think they have arrived. They no longer struggle, their eyes are dulled, and the child within is dead:

> God says: I like youngsters. I want people to be like them.
> I don't like old people unless they are still children.
> I want only children in my Kingdom;
> This has been decreed from the beginning of time.
> Youngsters—twisted, humped, wrinkled, white-bearded—
> all kinds of youngsters, but youngsters.
> There is no changing it; it has been decided.
> There is room for no one else.
>
> I like little children
> because my image has not yet been dulled in them.
> They have not botched my likeness;
> They are new, pure, without a blot, without a smear.
> So, when I gently lean over them, I recognize myself in them.
>
> I like them because they are still growing,
> they are still improving.
> They are on the road, they are on their way.
> But with grown-ups there is nothing to expect any more.
> They will no longer grow, no longer improve.
> They have come to a full stop.
>
> It is disastrous—grown-ups thinking they have arrived.
>
> I like youngsters because they are still struggling. . . .

I like youngsters because of the look in their eyes. . . .

Alleluia! Alleluia! Open, all of you, little old [people]!
It is I, your God, the Eternal, risen from the dead,
     Coming to bring back to life the child in you.
Hurry! Now is the time. I am ready to give you again
     The beautiful face of a child, the beautiful eyes of a
     child.
For I love youngsters, and I want everyone to be like
     them.[3]

To Be Childlike

1. Keep recording in your journal your development in childlikeness. That is the spiritual yardstick that will help you check on your growth.

2. Choose a Bible passage about spiritual growth: Psalm 92:12-15; Colossians 3:12-17; 2 Thessalonians 1:3-4; 1 Peter 2:1-5; 2 Peter 3:18. Print it on a card and carry it in your pocket until you know it.

3. Read all the Scriptures suggested above. What qualities of Christian character are mentioned. Do you seek to grow in these qualities?

4. What opportunities are available for spiritual growth through your church? In what do you participate? Worship service, church school, prayer meetings, small groups, accountability relationships, personal spiritual mentors?

5. According to Luke 2:52, the child Jesus grew mentally, physically, spiritually, socially. How can you work toward well-rounded growth? What "growing pains" do you experience in any of these areas?

8

Compassion

MARK, age ten, had brought the family hammock to our church school picnic. He strung it between two trees and went off to play with his friends.

When Mark returned, he found a little girl swinging peacefully in his hammock. At that age he demonstrated his fondness for little girls by assuming a he-man attitude. "That's my hammock, see? You're trespassing on my property, see? You know people can get arrested for that?"

The little girl tumbled out of the hammock, looking as scared as Mark hoped she would. I saw her walk away a short distance, then turn to watch Mark stretch out in his hammock. She paused, then came forward timidly. "May I swing you?" she asked.

Mark endured about ten seconds of her gentle swinging. Then he hopped out of the hammock and shouted to her as he ran away, "I just remembered, I got to meet some guys. You swing all you want to."

The little girl was rewarded with unlimited hammock privileges. Did she offer to swing Mark as a trick to gain that privilege? No, a childlike compassion is not manipulative. If I show compassion and love to get some benefit for myself, I am no longer childlike.

The story of the little slave girl who sent Naaman, the leper, for healing is one of many "unfinished" Bible stories. What happened to that child, God's instrument of compassion? Did she become a cherished daughter in that adoptive home?

Children are sensitive to a lack of compassion in adults, especially in those they have come to respect as role models. Children know no prejudice until we teach them.

A retreat leader related an incident from her childhood, and I tell it with her permission.

Heidi's father was a respected and beloved family doctor in a small town. Calls for help, some serious, some trivial, often interrupted the family dinner. Heidi unquestioningly accepted her father's ideals of service to the community. They were a Christian family.

One day the family was driving home from an out-of-town visit. The road took them through a nearby Indian reservation. An Indian woman was thumbing a ride toward town. To Heidi's surprise, her father drove by without stopping.

"Why didn't we stop and give that lady a ride?" asked Heidi.

Her mother brushed the question aside. "Oh, she could have lice or something."

Alone in the backseat, five-year-old Heidi sobbed

quietly. She sensed but could not verbalize that she had just witnessed an inconsistency in her parents, a prejudice, a lack of compassion.

Sophia was about fifteen months old when the family flew to Alabama to visit friends. During the visit, she was sick. On the flight home to Pennsylvania, Sophia, unhappy and cranky, tried the patience of her parents. Her father finally became exasperated with her.

Big brother Jesse, four years old, turned to his father and said, "Daddy, she's tired, and she's hungry, and she just wants somebody to hold her gently and not yell at her."

How often a child's compassion exceeds our expectations!

Joseph's family had volunteered to prepare a health kit that their church was sponsoring for an overseas relief project. Joseph's parents wanted to involve their three-year-old son in the project. Would he save enough money to buy a bar of soap for the kit? They placed a little coin bank in the bathroom. When Joseph washed his hands, he would be reminded to save soap money for a child who had none.

One evening when he was getting ready for bed, Joseph asked, "Daddy, does that little boy have sparkly toothpaste like I have?"

"No," father replied, "it's not likely that a boy who needs soap has toothpaste."

"And does he have a towel, Daddy? And does water come out of his sink?"

How far does my compassion extend as I seek to become childlike?

"That's not fair!" How often we hear that expression from children at play. They are sensitive to fairness, and they look to us for consistency in words and actions. Jesus warned "Why do you call me 'Lord, Lord,' and do not do what I tell you?" (Luke 6:46).

In a radio interview, author Elie Wiesel commented that children can learn to hate by the age of three. We are not born with hatred, he said. We learn to hate. So children by the age of three learn to hate when they see examples of hatred in people they live with.

Little children have this open doorway into the nature of the kingdom. Until we confuse them with our prejudices, they possess an innate sensitivity to spiritual consistency and fairness.

Heidi's introduction to prejudice reminds me of an incident from my preschool childhood. Because we lived on a busy city street, I was confined to the fenced-in backyard to play.

The only neighborhood child my age was Buddy, several houses away. Buddy was allowed the freedom of the back alley, and he came to my gate. My mother found us happily digging together in my little garden pile of dirt.

Buddy was ushered out of the gate, and I was ushered into the house. My mother's only comment was "Just wait until I tell your daddy when he comes home."

I didn't know what I was waiting for. I remember the scene as being literally "on the carpet." My father entered the kitchen door, where a long strip of rag carpet extended from the door to the kitchen sink. I stood by the sink.

"Guess what Grace did today," said my mother. "She played with a BOY!"

At that age, having only an older sister, I had no idea what made me a girl and Buddy a boy. The culture of my parents ruled that nice little girls don't play with little boys. That experience taught me prejudice and started me on the way to a confused sense of my own sexuality.

Happy the child who is free to express compassion, a sense of what is fair, without the self-consciousness that adult prejudices impose.

Justin, age three, sat near me in the small country church. "This is a dreary morning," said the worship leader. "Let's brighten it up by turning around and shaking hands with our neighbors."

Justin sat in the front row with his grandmother. Unnoticed by her, he slipped into the row behind her and moved across, shaking hands with each person. He turned into the next row, stepping carefully across feet and around knees, continuing to shake hands with each person. He finished the last pew on the left side, then moved across to the last pew on the right side.

The worship leader announced, "I guess we'll go on with the service even if Justin isn't finished."

Justin continued across each row on the right, from back to front. Neighbors and visitors alike all got a courteous handshake from the solemn little tow-headed boy. Justin didn't say a word. He just acted out his own sense of fairness. Everyone deserved his attention and handshake.

Karen and a friend, both age ten, stood watching the pen of colored Easter chicks for sale in a variety store downtown. They saw that one chick was the object of torment. Others pecked at him until he could no longer stand up. Leaving her friend to guard the injured chick, Karen ran home, almost a mile, to get money.

They pointed out to the salesperson the chick they wanted to buy. "Do you know that chicken is sick?" asked the clerk. "It can't even stand up."

"We know. That's why we want it," the girls explained. "We want to protect it and help it get well." They left the store, cradling the sick chicken.

To be childlike is to demonstrate a loving unself-conscious response to the hurts and needs of others.

Once we were attending a dedication service for a chapel just completed by the student members of a Christian community. This community's pledge is to turn away no one of any age who comes and is willing to seek a new life in commitment to Jesus Christ.

Its student population often reaches forty. Some seek to break long drug and alcohol addictions. Some are offenders whom area judges parole to the community. Some suffer psychological disorders.

Here they have learned to share community responsibilities, growing and preserving food, cutting firewood for heat, tending animals raised for food, building and maintaining the buildings.

The new chapel was a simple structure, still without furniture. We sat on the concrete floor for the service of dedication. Kevin, a student, sang a solo, "Blessed Assurance, Jesus Is Mine." Kevin was going to be "graduated" from the community the following week.

While a part of this community, Kevin had experienced that blessed assurance as a liberating reality. He had conquered a long-standing drug habit. He had dealt with the fact that he tested HIV positive for AIDS. Now he was ready to move on and invest the rest of his life into ministering to others sunk in the pits from which he had been rescued.

Kevin sang with the passion and free abandon typical of black gospel singers. Many of us were wiping tears from our eyes. As he ended the song, he burst into loud sobs. His six-foot frame shook as he slid to the floor and wept. The audience was hushed.

A little girl, the daughter of a worker in the community, slipped away from her mother, ran across the floor, and threw herself into Kevin's arms. Kevin clasped her in his arms and gradually his sobs abated. The child returned quietly to her mother.

That child knew how to show compassion. And she did not hesitate to do it. I wished that I, too, could have so spontaneously expressed my compassion for

Kevin. I believe others in the group felt that way, too. The child acted for all of us.

Another quality of childlike love is the child's ability to forgive, and to love unconditionally. We've all heard children going through disagreements at play. They may say, "I'm never going to play with you again." They pick up their toys and go home. A half hour later, they're playing together again, the dispute forgotten.

Arlan was displaying the usual two-year-old's rebellion at parental authority. His parents had a "naughty chair." When he disobeyed, Arlan had to sit on the naughty chair for some assigned minutes. Sometimes he struggled, cried, and shouted "No! No!" But he had disobeyed, they had warned, and they enforced the naughty chair.

Arlan found his own way of letting them know when the discipline had done its work. He would start to sing, "Mommy (or Daddy) loves me, this I know, for the Bible tells me so."

Sometimes parents discipline in anger, sometimes unjustly. Even then, children may express love when the parent is at fault. A boy had spilled his red fruit drink on the tan carpet. His mother lashed out at him angrily. Later, she regretted her hasty action. It had been an accident. She apologized. The boy said, "That's okay. I love you when you're good and when you're bad."

How disarming the love of children can be! Jared at age four was ingenuous at inventing excuses to delay bedtime. One evening he came downstairs to complain that his little sister was talking too much. Then he needed a drink. Five minutes later he appeared again, saw disapproval on his parents' faces, and explained, "I just had to go to the bathroom." He heard threats of punishment if he came downstairs one more time.

A few minutes later, they heard footsteps approaching the stairs. Father picked up a ruler from the desk and waited. Jared came to the door and appraised the situation. He hesitated a moment, smiled, and said, "I just forgot to kiss you good-night, Daddy."

The childlike spirit of love and compassion does not die easily, even when the child has been negatively impacted by our society.

In a class of nine-to-eleven-year-old boys, Jackie was my discipline problem Number One. The family lived around the corner from the church. He and his two younger brothers received little parental care. They were growing up on the streets. Each parent worked a different shift. So the parent at home, usually wanting to sleep, sent the boys outdoors.

Jackie's father died suddenly of a heart attack. In less than three months, his mother had remarried. Now it seemed as if each church school session presented a challenge to Jackie. How could he attract attention to himself and disrupt the class? In the middle of the Bible study, he might say, "Hey, guys, look. Mark has a pocket full of pancakes!"

As I prayed one day, I believe the Lord directed my mind. Jackie's name was John. What did that suggest to me? John—the disciple whom Jesus loved! Surely that was Jackie's greatest need, to know he was loved.

The next Sunday, when I dismissed the children, I took a firm grip on Jackie's arm and asked him to stay. I wanted to talk to him. He expected a scolding and would have run away if I hadn't held on.

I began to speak softly. "Jackie, I would like to call you John from now on." He scowled. Only his school-teacher called him John, and he didn't like it. But I continued.

"If my name were John, I would be really proud to have people call me John." He relaxed a bit, and I loosened my grip. "Do you remember that Jesus had a disciple named John? He was Jesus' best friend. Of course, Jesus loved every one of his disciples and all the other people he met, too. But Jesus loved John as a very close friend.

"With John, Jesus could share special secrets. Many times when the Bible mentions John, he is called 'the disciple whom Jesus loved.' If my name were John, I think that every time someone called me John, I would whisper to myself, 'I am the one Jesus loves.' "

Jackie looked into my eyes. His face was saying something for which he had no words. Then he dashed out the door.

For a week I wondered and prayed. The next Sunday, Jackie arrived with a camera. It was his mother's, he said. He wanted me to put it in a safe place until church school had ended.

I sensed a different atmosphere in my class. No, Jackie did not suddenly become a model of obedience. But when I saw mischief looming, I directed some question or pointed remark to him, addressing him as John. His eyes would twinkle a message that seemed to say to me, "We have a wonderful secret, haven't we?" And he made an honest effort to behave.

When the class was dismissed, I learned why he had brought the camera. He asked me to come outside the church with him so he could take my picture! Jackie was telling me had gotten the message. He knew he was loved. He could dare to love, also.

To Be Childlike

1. This week seek to be sensitive to inconsistencies in your own life that reveal a lack of compassion.

2. What are the prejudices in your life? Try to trace them back to their roots so they can be grubbed out.

3. Jesus accepted the company of tax collectors and prostitutes. He showed love for them. Who is the outcast, the less-than-desirable neighbor or church member? How can you show compassion? Will you choose to sit next to that person in church?

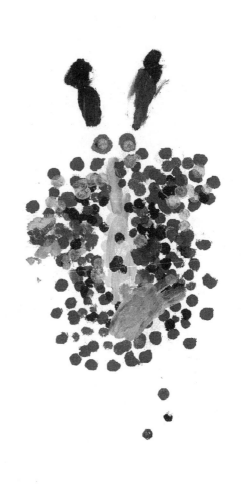

No Masks

DANNY'S life crossed mine for about two hours one morning. He left an unforgettable mark. I had chosen to walk to the bank about a mile away. The neighborhood consisted of shabby row houses, many converted to apartments.

By the gate stood a tear-stained little boy, perhaps four or five years old. My brisk pace slowed as I glimpsed his woebegone face. Our eyes met, and I said "Hi."

"Do you know why I'm crying?"

Those words stopped me in my tracks. I took in the surroundings; a walkway leading to the gate came from a rear door, probably a small first-floor apartment. Four steps led from the pavement to the gate, so the child and I stood eye to eye.

"Do you know why I am crying?" His face was naked pain. I couldn't go on without listening to his "Why."

"'Cause my Mommy went to work," he sobbed.

First I needed to determine that someone was there

caring for him. He told me that Jeannie took care of him. Jeannie was in the house. But he was sad without his mommy.

He talked on, and I listened. His name was Danny. "Mommy needed to go to work to get money," he said, "money to buy food and clothes for me."

I admired his new sneakers and jeans. "Your Mommy must love you lots and lots to buy such nice clothes for you," I assured him. He turned his rear to me and proudly patted the name patch on the pocket of his jeans.

"My mommy will always come back," Danny continued. "When she's done working, she'll come back."

I could envision a mother parting from weeping Danny, feeding him those promises to stem his tears and fears.

"I believe your mommy will always come back to you, Danny," I reassured him. "It's all right to feel sad when your mommy goes to work. And it's all right to cry sometimes when you feel sad. When I feel sad, I cry, too."

His eyes riveted on mine, absorbing a new thought. I offered him a tissue from my pocket. He mopped his eyes, blew his nose, and returned it to me with a polite "thank-you."

The encounter seemed to have ended, and I continued walking to the bank.

I walked more slowly, though, looking intently at the faces of passersby. In the bank I looked at the people waiting in teller lines. Many faces seemed to show stress and pain. Many more appeared to be shut up tight, determined to let nothing show. How many, I wondered, had long ago given up any such calling out: "Do you know why I am crying?"

Twenty minutes later, I was returning home by the same route. Danny still stood by the gate. He was no longer crying, but he looked small and alone and forlorn. I smiled to him as I approached. Then for the second time, he asked a question that snared me.

"Will you come and sit with me for awhile?"

"My daddy (husband) is waiting for me at home." I began to give that excuse and hated having spoken it even as I heard the words coming from my mouth. Hastily I added, "But I will come and sit with you for awhile."

We sat together on the top step, Danny and I. We talked about red trucks and yellow cars that passed. We talked more about Mommy going to work, probably as a waitress. Danny confided that he would like to go with Mommy to work, but he would be a bad boy and make noise, and they wouldn't like that.

"I don't believe you would be a bad boy," I said. "Maybe when you play you make noise. Maybe some people where Mommy works don't like noise. But that doesn't mean you're a bad boy."

Once more his eyes searched mine. He wanted to hear again the assurances from the first encounter and imprint the new ones. And he repeated them aloud: "My mommy loves me, and she will always come home again.

"It's all right to be sad when Mommy goes to work.

"It's all right to cry sometimes when I'm sad.

"It's all right to make noise sometimes, and I'm not a bad boy."

As he made each of these statements, I fed them back to him, affirming with my voice, my words, my smile, my nods. "Yes, it's all right, Danny. It's all right. . . ."

We sat silently for awhile. Then Danny looked at me, and seriously he stated, "Your daddy is waiting for you to come home."

He was releasing me, letting me know that the encounter had done its healing, that he could handle it now.

Somewhere in the process of growing up, we begin to design masks to disguise our true feelings. We build up walls around us so that we can hide away with our hurts. Perhaps we have been shamed or ridiculed.

"Big boys don't cry over a little bump."

"A good Christian shouldn't feel hurt about criticism."

"You shouldn't be angry because a friend betrayed a confidence."

So we conclude that it's not safe to let our true feelings hang out. We determine never to be vulnerable again. As adults we become, according to Ashley Montagu, "deteriorated children." We panic at the thought of exposing our weaknesses and fears.[1]

The masks we wear, the walls we raise for protection, can eventually become prisons that constrict our growth. Instead of admitting that I am crying inside, I react with resentment toward others who seem to be happy. I am critical, judgmental toward those who should know that I'm hurting but don't seem to care.

Eventually I can deceive even myself. That may result in depression. I shut down feelings at a deep inner level. Personhood is deteriorating.

To become childlike means to be vulnerable, even at the risk of being hurt. It means to admit my feelings honestly to myself, to appropriate others at appropriate times.

"To live with a mask," says Gayle Erwin in *The Jesus Style*, "is not to experience the freedom of the Spirit who administers forgiveness and gives us courage to rip the veil aside and reflect God's glory."[2]

Sometimes I need to risk asking, "Do you know why I am crying?" But before I ask that question, I need to be in touch with my own feelings and be honest with myself and with God about what I feel. It's easy to fall into a trap of playing games with myself that keep the feelings buried. But they are always buried alive.

Danny's second request on that memorable day made me aware that when we listen to them, children can often tell us what they need and what we can do about it. Danny's request was simple and direct, not unreasonable or unrealistic. "Will you come and sit with me for awhile?"

I couldn't bring his mommy home from work. He didn't ask for that. He just asked me to sit with him, to be present to him. And he wisely let me know when my presence had done its healing work.

The childlike Christian knows how meaningful such Presence can be, when God is consoling us through others:

> The God of all consolation . . . consoles us in all our affliction, so that we may be able to console those who are in any affliction with the consolation with which we ourselves are consoled by God. For just as the sufferings of Christ are abundant for us, so also our consolation is abundant through Christ. (2 Cor. 1:3-5)

This is the Jesus Christ who has promised to be with us "always, to the end of the age" (Matt. 28:20). He is the "king" who urges us to welcome and care for strangers (25:34-40), and thus to share that healing Presence.

Occasionally I have hesitated to go to someone in deep suffering. What could I say? I have learned that sometimes it is enough just to go and to say by words or actions, "I care about you and want to be close to you for awhile." Danny taught me that lesson.

I remember with gratitude the gift of Presence from others. I remember a friend who drove a hundred miles to sit at the hospital with me while my husband underwent serious spinal surgery.

A great biblical drama stresses the value of Presence. Job's three friends came and sat on his ash heap with him for seven days and nights before they spoke. Their comforting seems to have ended when they opened their mouths. After listening to two cycles of their speeches, Job cried out, "Listen carefully to my words, and let this be your consolation. Bear with me, and I will speak; then after I have spoken, mock on" (Job 21:1-3).

Even the Lord Jesus did not hesitate to express his need for Presence when he faced the cross. To the inner circle of three disciples, he said, "I am deeply grieved, even to death; remain here, and stay awake with me."

His friends let him down. They fell asleep. They deserved the Lord's rebuke. "So, could you not stay awake with me one hour?" (Matt. 26:36-45).

One Saturday morning, I entered our little country church. I needed to make some preparations for church school class next day.

As I passed through the rear of the sanctuary to go upstairs, I saw a woman sitting there alone. She was a casual acquaintance. I felt a burden for her as I finished my chores. Should I speak to her? Should I exit and allow her the solitude she had sought?

When I reentered the sanctuary, I went and sat down beside her and said softly, "May I sit with you for awhile?"

How long did we sit there without speaking? Perhaps for half an hour. I prayed silently for her, for whatever burden had brought her there.

Suddenly she began to sob and to pour out a story

of shattered family relationships. My experience with Danny had taught me the value of Presence, of simply sitting with the hurting one.

Marcia is another small child who has taught me to express my feelings and ask for my needs. Marcia was five, a foster child, a ward of the county. More than five years of worldly-wise experience seemed to be pooled in her dark eyes. I sensed that she struggled with feelings for which she had no words or even concepts to express.

Each week I picked up Marcia and three other foster children of that family for church school. Since the worship service came before the church school hour, I assumed responsibility for these four children during worship. We had no nursery or children's program during that hour.

Marcia was obviously having an unhappy morning even as she got into my car. The worship service loomed long and difficult. My coloring books, games, and puzzles held no appeal. Even the candy packet was only a minute's diversion.

I took Marcia's piquant small face between my hands, looked into her eyes, and whispered, "Marcia, what do you need to make you happy today?"

She hesitated only a moment, then whispered in my ear, "I need to sit on your lap."

I gathered her into my arms and held her close. Her small arm slipped around my neck. I touched my cheek to her soft one. Then her face nestled down into my neck.

All through the worship service, she scarcely moved, except to express with a tug here or a hug there that she needed a tighter embrace. Whatever Marcia's needs were that morning, they were satisfied or at least made bearable by the warmth of contact love.

I have met crises in my life when there was no human being who could be Presence to me. As a childlike member of my heavenly Parent's family, I have learned to admit to him, "I need to sit on your lap." And God has held me close. This helped to make all the confusions and discontents of daily living bearable again.

We had as houseguests a family with several small boys. I had risen early to prepare a pancake breakfast. Frankie, the youngest, popped into the kitchen almost immediately. After good-morning hugs and kisses, he sat at the table, awaiting his pancakes and entertaining me with his chatter.

I looked up to see Marlin, an older boy, about seven, come drooping glumly down the stairs. He clutched his security blanket in one fist and trailed it behind him, with the thumb of his other hand jammed into his mouth. He looked disconsolate.

As I looked at Marlin, I invited, "Here I am waiting with a big good-morning hug that I need to give away to someone."

Immediately little Frankie hopped up, flung his arms wide, and said, "You can have me!"

It took some gentle maneuvering to satisfy Frankie

and get beyond him to Marlin, who couldn't express his needs.

To be childlike means to be aware of the heavenly Father waiting patiently with outstretched arms of steadfast love. It means letting go of the sham security of my blanket and thumb, and opening wide my empty arms to him: "You can have me, Lord!"

To Be Childlike

1. Are you playing games with yourself to hide your feelings from yourself? Try to get in touch with feelings, and record them in your journal.

2. Be aware of the masks you wear to hide your feelings from others. Is there some appropriate person, at an appropriate time, to whom you can express those feelings? Can they be expressed in ways that do not harm yourself or others?

3. Do not be afraid of others who express feelings. Do not back away from them.

4. Risk being Presence to someone who may be waiting for you to come and sit for awhile. Be content to be Presence without yielding to advising, admonishing, or judging.

Creativity

ELIZABETH, age three, showed me a handful of marbles. She chose four and placed them in my hand. "Two of these are white, and two are milky-white," I commented.

"Do you know that milk is a cow's ornament?" Elizabeth informed me. What was she expressing? I think she was telling me that milk is important in her world, and it is the cow who ornaments her life with milk.

Paul wrote to the Colossians, "Let your conversation be always gracious, never insipid; and study how best to talk with each person you meet" (Col. 4:6, NEB).

Nathan, four years old, was telling his mother about a special friend at church school. "Whenever I think about Calbert, I think about those potatoes that are really soft and don't have any skins."

Do we let our speech, especially speech about spiritual things, become insipid, trite clichés? Small children show creativity in speech. We haven't yet stuffed them so full of conventional expressions as to wipe out their creativity. Milk may still be a cow's ornament. A friend may still be described as warm and comfortable as mashed potatoes.

A friend was spending overnight with a brother's family. She appeared for breakfast, wearing her housecoat.

Her small nephew said, "Aunt Laura, you have a pretty Good Morning!"

His mother explained that Good Morning was the name he had created for a housecoat. Good childlike logic, wasn't it? Mother usually appeared in the morning wearing her housecoat, and said, "Good morning, Jimmy." So the housecoat was her Good Morning.

We don't limit creativity to words. When I'm driving alone, I sometimes sing Scriptures that I know by memory. I try to make my impromptu tunes fit the words. I doubt that anyone but the Lord would appreciate my musical improvisations. But I believe they keep me headed toward more childlike creativity.

A little girl wanted to wear new clothes the following day. Her mother said, "Yes, if it doesn't rain."

"Then I'll pray that the sun will shine."

Father got into the conversation. "I was praying it would rain tomorrow. My garden is dry and needs water. What will God do now?"

The child hesitated only a moment, then smiled confidently. "I guess then God will send a rainbow."

A child's original birthday greeting tops any that the store racks provide. Naomi, about seven, sent this to me. Here is the text of it, complete with her spellings (whole quotation sic):

"Dear Aunt Grace and Uncle George. I was sick yeterday day. and my friends house just burt down. happy birthday any way. I love you. Naomi."

We nurture creativity when we give the children drawing materials and blank paper. They need opportunity to express their own ideas in art. We stifle creativity when we give them only coloring books and expect them to color only within the lines. Let them be creative colorers!

Children in my kindergarten class at church were illustrating scenes from the Christmas story. I paused to look at Bobby's drawing of angels singing to the shepherds. Two figures hovered in the sky. I said, "You drew two angels, Bobby."

He corrected me: "No, that one is the devil."

I grasped the drama of what he had portrayed. His "angel" stood with a rod or sword pointed at the second figure. That one, his "devil" figure, was enclosed in a circle, kept encaged by the power of the angel.

We had not mentioned the evil influences at work when Christ was born, the children of Bethlehem slaughtered by Herod's orders. But it was there in the child's drawing, and the life of the Christ Child protected.

Creative expressions from children give us occasion for smiles. I believe the Lord enjoys those smiles, too, not just from children, but also from childlike adults. Jonathan's family was camping out for July 4 holiday. On Saturday evening they saw a spectacular fireworks display. At the end, the skies exploded with sound and color, and someone said, "That's the grand finale."

On Sunday morning they went to worship at a nearby church. The sermon was long. The speaker rose to an emotional crescendo, his voice getting louder and louder. Jonathan, five years old, whispered to his mother, "Is this the grand finale?"

It was raining hard one Sunday morning. The nine-to-eleven-year-olds in my class were disgruntled and complaining about the weather. I suggested that we try to think about the rain, its smells, its sounds, and so on. We pooled our ideas. The following poem was the result:

Rain is falling everywhere.
Rain is falling in my hair.
It brings a spring smell from the earth.
I hear the rain on the window, the prettiest sound,
It sounds like horses coming.
At the end of the rain comes the rainbow.
And I know God keeps his promises.
And I take off my shoes and walk barefoot
In wet grass and mud.

In a lighter vein, Marilynn gave me her essay entitled "Church," written when she was seven.

People like to go to church.
If we didn't have chairs to sit on,
what would we have to sit on?
If we didn't have clothes to wear,
how would we look on the way to church?
If we didn't have a watch,
how would we know what time to go to church?
If we didn't have a broom,
how would we keep the church clean?
If we didn't have a Bible
what would the preacher read to us?
If we didn't have no money,
What would we put in the offering?

Sometimes children astound me with the depth of their creativity. Naomi, at age eight, sent me her poem, "I Have a Dream."

I wish I could stop wars
because I hate to see people
lying on the street and dying.
Nobody leans down and helps them.
It makes me want to cry.

A more recent one of Naomi's creations is this:

I see the sunset light pink and light blue.
Together they create a lovely hue.
And as dark curtains begin to fall
A big dark veil covers all.
But I don't worry. For heaven's sake
The sun will be there when I awake.

Another child, in sixth grade, wrote about "The Flower and the Toad."

> I walked along a mountain road
> And saw a flower blooming there.
> Beside it hopped an ugly toad;
> It made the flower seem more fair.
>
> And yet I'm sure that in God's eyes
> There is no difference between the two.
> If we were just half as wise
> We might see them his way, too.

Children have taught me to look for fresh ways to express what Jesus and his kingdom mean to me. They sometimes trip me up with their perceptions. In my church school class with ten-year-olds, we were discussing the meaning of worship. I read to them from the lesson book, "We worship when we think about God."

Terry challenged me. "I often think about the devil, but that doesn't mean that I worship him." That's enough to keep a teacher on her toes, isn't it?

Those same children surprised me with their insights into Bible truths and their ability to express them. Our lesson was about God giving the Ten Commandments to Moses.

"What happens to someone who breaks the laws of our country or our state?" I asked.

Responses came quickly:

"They go to jail."

"They have to pay a fine."

"When they pay for their crimes, they're free again."

My next question was "What happens to us when we break God's laws?" I could see the struggle in their faces as they pondered that big question.

Michael broke the silence. "It's like you are in prison for your whole life! Inside of you!"

Yes, when we break God's laws, we break ourselves. No prison term or fine can satisfy and set us free. Only God in Jesus Christ can open the door to that prison inside us.

With third-graders in vacation Bible school, I brought a large poster with these letters at the top: GOD IS. . . . I asked the children to add their perceptions of who God is.

They wrote the following: Love, Helper, Kind, Good, Generous and Gentle, Answers prayer, Feeds us, Provides, Helps needy and homeless, Forgives, Cares, Helps us grow, Listens, Creates us, Gives light, Heals, Miracle worker, Gives trees, Keeps promises, Knows what we think, Gives us homes, Gives happiness and joy, Gives us church, Gave us the Bible.

The technological explosion in the toy department is stifling creativity in our children. Is it doing the same to us as adults? The six-year-old who needs a video game may have lost the challenge of building a dream kingdom with blocks.

The doll that drinks and burps and wets a diaper no longer satisfies the child who wants a doll that speaks and plays pat-a-cake. The child with a homemade rag doll and a creative mind has a doll that can do anything she can imagine it to do.

Richard Foster in, *Celebration of Discipline*, wrote,

Let us with abandon relish the fantasy games of children. Let's see visions and dream dreams. Let's play, sing, laugh. The imagination can release a flood of creative ideas, and exercising our imagination can be lots of fun. Only those who are insecure about their own maturity will fear such a delightful form of celebration.[1]

To Be Childlike

1. The psalmists used many creative expressions to describe God, to attest to his unfailing availability to them. Read through some psalms, looking for descriptive images of who God is and what he does. Then write your own contemporary comparisons such as these:

• God is my travel guide, with the maps carefully marked.

• God is my safe storm shelter when thunder roars and lightning flashes.

• God is the never-failing flashlight when electric power fails.

2. Write your own version of Psalm 23. David had faithfully guarded his sheep. Out of his own experience, he wrote, "The Lord is my Shepherd. . . ." What

is your present role or occupation? Following David's thought patterns, write your own psalm, starting something like these:

- The Lord is my Writing Instructor. . . .
- The Lord is my School Administrator. . . .
- The Lord is my Senior Pastor. . . .
- The Lord is my Physician, my Psychiatrist. . . .
- The Lord is my Best Friend. . . .

These exercises may be both serious and playful. Playfulness is a childlike characteristic. I believe the Lord enjoys a playful spirit in us.

A Child Draws People into Community

IN October 1987, in Midland, Texas, an eighteen-month-old child fell down a well shaft. For about sixty hours, rescuers worked round the clock, drilling through solid rock to try to reach the child. The whole nation waited anxiously.

On a Friday evening at eight o'clock, three major television networks interrupted prime-time shows to televise the successful completion of the rescue.

Was there something special about that little girl? War raged on in Afghanistan. African refugees were starving. But it was the plight of one little child trapped in a well shaft that drew a nation into a community of concern.

A new neighbor with a small baby told me that she thought our town was unusually friendly. She and her baby had gone grocery shopping. Several people had stopped to talk with her.

On a subsequent shopping trip without the baby, she found that people attended to their own shopping needs and she was ignored.

What made the difference? The presence of a little child!

Jesse's mother took him for a haircut. The two younger children, Sophia and Daphne, were with her. The little girls played and laughed and ran around the waiting area.

Others were in the waiting room. The mother admitted she was getting rather frazzled, trying to keep the girls from annoying others.

As they were ready to leave, an older man laid his hand on the mother's arm and said, "I just have to tell you, you have wonderful children." With tears in her eyes, the mother thanked him. The children had not been an annoyance, but a delight.

I remember a long-ago scene in a restaurant a few weeks before Christmas. My sister and I were shopping together for a few gifts. Her daughter Lois, nineteen months old, was with us.

The morning drizzle had turned to sleet and then to snow. Shoppers were scarce. The weather seemed to have settled into a full-blown snowstorm by the time we stopped at a restaurant for lunch.

Near the end of our meal, someone put a coin in the jukebox. "Winter Wonderland" began to play. Lois loved music, and she loved to dance. She scrambled to her feet on her high chair and began her version of dancing. Her feet didn't move, but all the rest of her body did, shoulders and tummy and hips and hands and head moved with the music.

As Lois danced, I noticed the slim, maroon-sweatered man nearby. His face turned toward Lois was a mass of wrinkles, laugh wrinkles. His gaze never left the little dancer. His wrinkles deepened, and his eyes were crescents of twinkling delight.

The music ended, and Lois returned to her dessert. But the waitress who had paused at the man's table went directly to the jukebox and inserted another coin.

Lois climbed to her feet for her second performance. The man began a staccato beat with his feet. His arms were folded on the table, his eyes on the child, his food forgotten. Lois turned toward the man. His ageless blue eyes and her dark brown ones spoke to each other across the room. She danced to him, and he tapped to her.

Taking her station by the jukebox, the waitress kept the music flowing. The drama drew more spectators. Two businessmen deserted the sheaf of papers between them and ate their pie slowly as they watched the child. A gray-haired man and woman eased their chairs around for a better view.

Waitresses enjoyed the lull. They stood at the side-lines smiling their answers to customer comments. The restaurant kitchen was glass enclosed. Three kitchen workers stood by the glass partition and watched.

Lois's mother finished the last bit of ice cream in the child's dish, and we prepared to leave. Helping to tug Lois into her snowsuit, I felt like a stagehand at a first-night performance.

The music ended. The clatter of dishes and hum of conversation resumed. But it had a different quality. The gray-haired woman was showing pictures from her wallet to one of the businessmen, and I heard her explaining about "our grandchildren in Texas."

As I paid our bill, the manager at the cash register wished me an unusually warm and friendly Merry Christmas.

Behind me, the businessman waited to pay. I heard him advise the manager, "For that kind of a floor show, you could slap on a cover charge."

"But that kind you can't buy," answered the manager.

As we left the restaurant, Lois leaned over her mother's shoulder, waved to the old man, the waitresses, and all the patrons. "Bye," she called to them all.

Outdoors, the snow pelting me couldn't quell the warmth I felt inside. The warmth radiating from people who had allowed a little child to draw them into community. I thought of the peaceable kingdom prophesied by Isaiah, who said, "A little child shall lead them" (Isa. 11:9).

It goes beyond coincidence that one holiday does more than any other to draw people into loving relationships and expressions of caring. It is the one celebrating the birth of the Holy Child.

Beyond all the glitter and gaudy performance, there

is a show that money cannot buy. Staged in a stable, accompanied by an angel choir, it centers on the tiny Baby, the Son of God, Emmanuel. This child holds the power to draw us closer to each other, closer to God.

In his account of South American travels in *"!Gracias!"* Henry Nouwen tells of living with children after many years of functioning only in the young adult academic world.

> After all my experiences with psychotherapy, I suddenly have discovered the great healing power of children. . . . I marvel at their ability to be fully present to me. Their uninhibited expression of affection and their willingness to receive it pulls me directly into the moment and invites me to celebrate life where it is found. . . . I now realize that only when I can enter with the children into their joy will I be able to enter also with them into their poverty and pain. God obviously wants me to walk into the world of suffering with a little child on each hand.[1]

The Mennonite reported the following, reprinted from *Mennonite Weekly Review*:

> The secret negotiations that led to last September's Israeli-Palestine Liberation Organization agreement took place in a country mansion south of Oslo, Norway. The hosts were two married couples. A four-year-old child played with his toys at the

feet of the negotiators. The Israelis and Palestinians, who are fond of children, gradually relaxed. They told jokes, and soon everyone was laughing."[2]

On Thursday, June 29, 1995, two little boys in Lima, Ohio, decided to "make waves." *The Lima News* reported that the boys, ages ten and eight, stood at a busy street corner, waving to motorists. By 4:20 p.m., people in a thousand vehicles had waved back to them.

The newspaper reported it as "a valid study in human nature. The boys said only ten people didn't wave back, and one returned their waves with an obscene gesture." One woman was in tears when she stopped her car to tell the boys that they had made her day.[3]

The story was picked up by Associated Press and recounted on National Public Radio, CBS radio, and CNN. Then came a phone call inviting the Wavers to appear on the *Tonight Show* with Jay Leno.

Can I become an example of childlikeness? Can the Lord Jesus, through changes in my life, draw others into a caring Christian community?

In prayer time in a small group, will I risk praying with the open simplicity of a child talking with a loving Father?

If I live out humility in my Christian life, if I sometimes allow myself to be dependent on others, I may risk removing my mask. In touch with my own feelings and needs, I may help others to reach out in expressions of Christian community. And maybe others also will open themselves and share.

If I have expressed my awe and wonder at God's Creation and continued working, will others be drawn with me into wonder and adoration?

The exercise of such childlike qualities will result in a desire to grow. It will help me to get in touch with levels of creativity in myself that have been buried beneath conventional, formal, conformist, unoriginal, rigid, and stereotyped expressions of my life in Christ.

As childlike Christians, we may be God's instruments to create new levels of community. Will *you* take some risks?

To Be Childlike

1. Have you sat in a doctor's waiting room when small children were present? Watch two toddlers who meet for the first time. They are curious about each other. They play with each other. They may even hug. The adults hide in their magazines. One adult introducing a topic of conversation with another, even with a stranger, may change the atmosphere of the waiting room, easing the tension. Try talking about the weather, some world or community news, and not about yourself or your symptoms.

2. While waiting in a checkout line, think of something positive to say to the checker. "I'm amazed at your skill in handling the computer checkout

machine." Or, "You've memorized prices on all the week's produce specials, haven't you?" Or, if all else fails, "I'm glad your store is so cheerful. There's always something interesting to look at while I wait."

3. Are there some in the church fellowship whose names you don't know or can't remember? Admit it to them. Try to imprint their names on your mind and call them by name when you meet again. Perhaps you can introduce them to someone else. It strengthens community.

4. Are you part of a small-group fellowship? Such groups foster community. In a Christian group, mutual trust, confidentiality, and accountability should gradually evolve. People should feel free to share both the depths of the pits that threaten them, and the joys that inspire dancing. Can you be the initiator of such a group? It does not require leadership skills. It does require that you express your own needs, longings, and joys. You can create a listening atmosphere where others may do the same. Make yourself vulnerable, childlike.

Listen to Your Inner Child

SOME Christians find it easy to acquire and practice the qualities of childlikeness which the Lord Jesus commended. Why do some of us find it so hard?

Why do I mask my feelings and dread becoming vulnerable? What hinders me from finding awe and wonder in the Lord and his Creation? What holds me back from reaching out to others with compassion and love? What stifles my creativity?

Some of us struggle to become childlike because experiences in early childhood robbed us of our childlikeness. Perhaps a child was never loved. A child may have experienced emotional or physical or sexual abuse.

Quarreling parents and their divorce rob a child of security. Creativity is stifled when a child is not permitted to fantasize or is ridiculed for creative play. When no one listens to a child, that child loses a magnetic quality that draws people into community.

I didn't have perfect parents, and neither did you. Even the most committed Christian parents sometimes make mistakes. Each of us can agree as we search our own childhood memories.

As a Christian, I do have one perfect heavenly Parent. No matter what scars I bear from a damaged childhood, the heavenly Father waits to lead me into healing and childlikeness. As I follow, he sometimes allows me to become the caring, nurturing parent to my own inner child.

In *Christo-Psychology*, Morton Kelsey says, "Just as we need compassion for children, we need it for those rejected parts of ourselves in order to redeem them."[1]

In another book, *Transcend*, Kelsey says, "A means of sharing concretely in spiritual reality is spending time with children, for in relating to them we contact our own inner child. It is often our hurt inner child, starving for affection, who causes us trouble as adults until we take time to nourish and love it."[2]

No, my parents were not perfect. I realize that they both grew up in less than perfect homes. They gave far more love and security to me and my older sister than either of them had known as children. My mother was orphaned at age twelve and became a household servant to strangers. She was not allowed to continue in school.

In my early childhood years, there were strict rules of morality, but little Christian influence. My parents retained church membership in my father's childhood church, an hour away. We attended communion service there, perhaps four times a year.

In a strong Pennsylvania-German culture, we always sang in German "Ich weiss einen Strom" (O Have You Not Heard of That Beautiful Stream). I liked to listen to it, but I didn't understand it. It seemed to me that communication with God had to be in a foreign language. At about age five, I was finally allowed to go to church school with my big sister.

The most painful period of childhood within my conscious memory was that my parents sent me to live with an aunt and uncle through the latter half of first grade. The reason stemmed from trauma, not in my own family, but in the home of the aunt and uncle. I was meant to be some kind of diversion for them while their adult daughter spent time in a mental institution.

When I went to live with them, my father told me, "You may not ask to come home until school is ended." I was only twenty miles from home and saw my family frequently. But each parting touched off a volcano of rejection and homesickness.

Another childhood incident was totally repressed in my subconscious. That did not surface until many years later, when my husband and I underwent training in psychotherapy. I had been sexually molested when I was a small child. The perpetrator remains unknown. It happened in a dark room, and I did not see the person who assaulted me.

As I worked through experiences of childhood, I

got in touch with this inner child and found healing. I believe that Jesus Christ transcends time and space. Unless that inner child would be healed and nurtured and loved, she would continue to influence my life as an adult. She interfered with my ability to develop relationships. She hindered my growth into the child-likeness that Jesus longed to see in me.

That hurting little child needed to be brought into the presence of Jesus. He was waiting to put his arms of love around my inner child, the part of me still hiding behind masks. He was saying to me, "Unless you become as a little child, you cannot enter the kingdom of God."

The repressed traumatic experiences of my early childhood stole from me much of the beauty of childhood, of childlike experiences. Buried in my subconscious, they buried alive much of the joyous and playful as well. Several times in dreams I have experienced reunions with the inner child. This has brought healing and direction.

My husband and I had attended a twelve-hour workshop guided by an internationally known psychiatrist, the late Dr. David Freundlich. The theme of the workshop was "Getting in Touch with Early Childhood Messages." Experiences of that day allowed me to move more deeply into some of those repressed pains.

That night I dreamed. I was seated beside my husband in a car as we drove down a narrow city street lined with row houses, the kind of neighborhood in which I had grown up. It was night. Suddenly the car lights shone on the figure of a little child, probably less than two years old, running wildly down the street. I shouted to my husband to stop the car.

I dashed out onto snow-covered ground and ran after the child. The child was barefoot and wore only a diaper. I reached the child, picked it up, and held it close to me. At first the child struggled. I was wearing a large, heavy coat. I opened the coat and wrapped the child inside, close to my body. I felt the struggles subside as it nestled in the warmth and security inside my coat, against my body.

The street was deserted. I reasoned that I needed to knock on doors and ask if anyone recognized the child. But before I could take that action, I awoke. Was the dream unfinished? No. I lay awake, still cherishing the feeling of the small body of the child held close to me. I knew that my own lost inner child had come to her true home within me.

An earlier dream was directional, when the child within the dream gave me wisdom for a major, life-changing decision. I was approaching marriage; that alone was life-changing, considering that I was more than fifty years old and had never been married.

My future husband taught at a church-related college and was faculty adviser to the Christian student group there. I was adviser to a Christian student group at a nearby college where I was registrar.

We were convinced that the Lord had a ministry for us as a couple, and we believed that it would be with students. We wanted to establish our home in a country setting that could become a retreat center for young people.

We investigated purchasing several plots of ground that seemed within our meager budget, prayed about each one, and saw something sour the deal each time. Questionable road rights, another buyer one day ahead of us, and so on.

My future husband lived in an apartment of an old row house, much like my childhood home. He mentioned to me that the house in which he lived was for sale, cheap, but we pursued it no further. We both wanted that plot of ground in the country where we could build a modest home.

Then came the night of the *dreams*. The setting for my dream was that old, shabby row house where I had lived as a child. I was approaching the kitchen door. A beautiful, bright-haired child ran joyfully to meet me. She clasped her arms around my knees in a hug of greeting and said, "Isn't this a beautiful day?"

I took her hand, and together we entered the kitchen. Then she added, "And isn't this a beautiful kitchen?"

I kneeled down so I could enter into her experience more fully at her own level. I held out my arms and embraced that spontaneously happy child.

"Yes, this is a beautiful day and a beautiful kitchen," I affirmed. "Thank you, Jesus, for this beautiful day and this beautiful kitchen."

I became aware of a Presence, someone standing

behind me. I felt hands placed on my head. I did not turn, did not move, but I knew that the Presence was the Lord Jesus. Raising my eyes, I could see the tips of the fingers of hands placed on my head. Then I awoke.

What was the message of that dream? As I lay awake and pondered, I realized that for the little child in the dream, the kitchen was beautiful. This was true not because of material surroundings, which were shabby, but because it was a place where she felt loved and cherished. I realized that when I had moved physically to her level, on my knees, I too could acknowledge its beauty. At that point, where I had become as a little child, I experienced the presence of Jesus. He laid his hands on me and blessed me.

I knew, then, that I could live with my husband in any house and be content. If the Lord wanted us in that old row house where he now lived, I was willing to go, and I knew it would be beautiful.

On that same night, my future husband had a dream, a short but vivid one: He stood in the kitchen of his apartment, the house that was for sale, and asked, "How can I ask my beloved to live in this miserable kitchen?"

The next day he told me his dream, and then I told him mine. His question was answered. We bought that old house and moved into it, not knowing what awaited us. Within a year, we became involved in a ministry of counseling which neither of us had anticipated, one to which that big old house was ideally suited.

I know that the child in my dream had revealed the wisdom and direction that we lacked, and for which we both had prayed.

To Be Childlike

1. Do you need to seek Jesus' healing for hurts to the child within you? Record in your journal the hurts that you remember.

2. Alone, in quietness, bring your hurting inner child to Jesus and ask in faith for his healing touch. He said, "Let the children come to me. Do not hinder them."

3. When memories of childhood trauma surface, be to that child a nurturing, loving parent. Would it help you to look at a photograph of yourself as a child?

4. Write a list of assurances that you may have longed to hear from your parents. List messages of love, security, and praise. Start feeding those positive messages to your inner child. The Number One message we all need to feed to our inner child is this: "You are special in the eyes of God. He loves you. God planned for you to be his special friend even before you were born."

5. To spend time in the company of children may give you permission to free the child within yourself.

6. Set your inner child free to restore to you the God-given wisdom of childlikeness.

Epilogue

Jesus and the Children

Matthew 19:13-15

Then little children were being brought to him in order that he might lay his hands on them and pray. The disciples spoke sternly to those who brought them; but Jesus said, "Let the little children come to me, and do not stop them; for it is to such as these that the kingdom of heaven belongs." And he laid his hands on them.

Luke 18:15-17

People were bringing even infants to him that he might touch them; and when the disciples saw it, they sternly ordered them not to do it. But Jesus called for them and said, "Let the little children come to me, and do not stop them; for it is to such as these that the kingdom of God belongs. Truly I tell you, whoever does not receive the kingdom of God as a little child will never enter it."

Mark 10:13-16

People were bringing little children to him in order that he might touch them; and the disciples spoke sternly to them. But when Jesus saw this, he was indignant and said to them, "Let the little children come to me; do not stop them; for it is to such as these that the kingdom of God belongs. Truly I tell you, whoever does not receive the kingdom of God as a little child will never enter it." And he took them up in his arms, laid his hands on them, and blessed them.

Matthew 18:1-7, 10-11, 14

At that time the disciples came to Jesus and asked, "Who is the greatest in the kingdom of heaven?" He called a child, whom he put among them, and said, "Truly I tell you, unless you change and become like children, you will never enter the kingdom of heaven. Whoever becomes humble like this child is the greatest in the kingdom of heaven. Whoever welcomes one such child in my name welcomes me.

"If any of you put a stumbling block before one of these little ones who believe in me, it would be better for you if a great millstone were fastened around your neck and you were drowned in the depth of the sea. Woe to the world because of stumbling blocks! Occasions for stumbling are bound to come, but woe to the one by whom the stumbling blocks come! . . .

"Take care that you do not despise one of these little ones, for, I tell you, in heaven their angels continually see the face of my Father in heaven. . . . So it is not the will of your Father in heaven that one of these little ones should be lost."

Luke 9:46-48

An argument arose among [the disciples] as to which one of them was the greatest. But Jesus, aware of their inner thoughts, took a little child and put it by his side, and said to them, "Whoever welcomes this child in my name welcomes me, and whoever welcomes me welcomes the one who sent me; for the least among all of you is the greatest."

Mark 9:31-37

He was teaching his disciples, saying to them, "The Son of Man is to be betrayed into human hands, and they will kill him, and three days after being killed, he will rise again." But they did not understand what he was saying and were afraid to ask him.

Then they came to Capernaum; and when he was in the house he asked them, "What were you arguing about on the way?" But they were silent, for on the way they had argued with one another who was the greatest. He sat down, called the twelve, and said to them, "Whoever wants to be first must be last of all and servant of all." Then he took a little child and put it among them; and taking it in his arms, he said to them, "Whoever welcomes one such child in my name welcomes me, and whoever welcomes me welcomes not me but the one who sent me."

Matthew 20:20-28

Then the mother of the sons of Zebedee came to him with her sons, and kneeling before him, she asked a favor of him. And he said to her, "What do you want?" She said to him, "Declare that these two sons of mine will sit, one at your right hand and one at your left, in your kingdom." But Jesus answered, "You do not know what you are asking. Are you able to drink the cup that I am about to drink?" They said to him, "We are able." He said to them, "You will indeed drink my cup, but to sit at my right hand and at my left, this is not mine to grant, but it is for those for whom it has been prepared by my Father."

When the ten heard it, they were angry with the two brothers. But Jesus called them to him and said, "You know that the rulers of the Gentiles lord it over them, and their great ones are tyrants over them. It will not be so among you; but whoever wishes to be great among you must be your servant, and whoever wishes to be first among you must be your slave; just as the Son of Man came not to be served but to serve, and to give his life a ransom for many."

Matthew 11:25-26

[Jesus lamented the apathy and indifference of towns in Galilee where he had ministered.] At that time Jesus said, "I thank you, Father, Lord of heaven and earth, because you have hidden these things from the wise and the intelligent and have revealed them to infants; yes, Father, for such was your gracious will."

Matthew 21:14-16

[Jesus made his Triumphal Entry into Jerusalem and cleansed the temple.] The blind and the lame came to him in the temple, and he cured them. But when the chief priests and the scribes saw the amazing things that he did, and heard the children crying out in the temple, "Hosanna to the Son of David," they became angry and said to him, "Do you hear what these are saying?" Jesus said to them, "Yes, have you never read, 'Out of the mouths of infants and nursing babes you have prepared praise for yourself'?"

Luke 22:24-27

[The disciples were at the Last Supper with Jesus.] A dispute also arose among them as to which one of them was to be regarded as the greatest. But he said to them, "The kings of the Gentiles lord it over them; and those in authority over them are called benefactors. But not so with you; rather the greatest among you must become like the youngest, and the leader like one who serves. For who is greater, the one who is at the table or the one who serves? Is it not the one at the table? But I am among you as one who serves."

Notes

Chapter 1: The Spiritual Life of the Child
1. Paul Tournier, *Learn to Grow Old* (London: SCM, 1971; New York: Harper & Row, 1986).
2. Albert Edward Day, *Autobiography of Prayer* (Nashville: Upper Room, 1979).

Chapter 2: Living in the World of the Spirit
1. Morton Kelsey, *Christianity as Psychology* (Minneapolis: Augsburg Publishing House, 1986).
2. Morton Kelsey, *The Christian and the Supernatural* (Minneapolis: Augsburg Publishing House, 1976).
3. Robert Coles, *The Spiritual Life of Children* (Boston: Houghton Mifflin, 1990).
4. Frances G. Wickes, *The Inner World of Childhood*, 3d ed. Inner World Ser. (Boston: Sigo, 1988 repr.).
5. Richard Foster, *Celebration of Discipline* (New York: Harper & Row, 1978).
6. Sofia Cavalletti, *The Religious Potential of the Child* (Mahwah, N.J.: Paulist Press, 1983).
7. Diane Komp, *A Window to Heaven* (Grand Rapids: Zondervan, 1992).
8. Children's Defense Fund, © 1998. Originally composed for National Children's Day, 1982. Used by permission.

Chapter 3: Prayer, Language of the Spiritual World
1. Richard J. Foster, op. cit.
2. James D. Burns, "Hushed Was the Evening," in *The Mennonite Hymnary* (Newton: Kan.: Faith & Life Press, 1940). Used by permission.

Chapter 4: Humility and Dependence
1. Richard Foster, op. cit.
2. Elton Trueblood, *The Company of the Committed* (New York: Harper & Row, 1961).

3. J. B. Phillips, *God Our Contemporary* (New York: Macmillan, 1960).
4. Foster, op. cit.

Chapter 5: Sense of Awe and Wonder
1. Morton Kelsey, *Reaching* (New York: Harper & Row, 1989).
2. Bruderhof Communities or the Society of Brothers, ed., *Children in Community* (Rifton, N.Y.: Plough Publishing, 1974). Used by permission.

Chapter 6: Simplicity
1. Robbie Trent, *Your Child and God* (New York: Harper & Brothers, 1941).
2. Maxie Dunham, *The Workbook on Spiritual Disciplines* (Nashville: Upper Room, 1984).

Chapter 7: Desire to Grow
1. Thomas Merton, *Contemplative Prayer* (Merton Legacy Trust, 1969).
2. Richard Foster, op. cit.
3. Michael Quoist, *Prayers*, trans. Agnes M. Forsyth and Anne Marie de Commaille (New York: © copyright Sheed and Ward, 1963), 3-5. Used by permission.

Chapter 9: No Masks
1. Ashley Montagu, *Growing Young*, 2d ed. (Westport, Conn.: Greenwood Publishing, 1988).
2. Gayle Erwin, *The Jesus Style* (Waco: Word Books, 1988).

Chapter 10: Creativity
1. Richard Foster, op. cit.

Chapter 11: A Child Draws People into Community
1. Henri Nouwen, *"¡Gracias!"* (New York: Harper & Row, 1987).
2. *The Mennonite* (Newton, Kan.), Aug. 23, 1994.
3. *The Lima News*, Lima Ohio, issues of 6/30/95 and 7/13/95.

Chapter 12: Listen to Your Inner Child
1. Morton Kelsey, *Christo-Psychology* (New York: Crossroad, 1982).
2. Morton Kelsey, *Transcend: A Guide to the Spiritual Quest* (New York: Crossroad, 1981).

The Author

Love for children has patterned much of the life of Grace Moyer Frounfelker, Bluffton, Ohio.

She began teaching in her first small home church in Allentown, Pennsylvania, with church school classes. Then she extended her teaching to summer camps, vacation Bible school, and neighborhood Bible clubs in her home and church.

For twelve years Frounfelker wrote children's church school curriculum for the General Conference Mennonite Church. She has published numerous devotional and inspirational articles.

Frounfelker is an accomplished storyteller for children and adult audiences and tells the children's story sometimes in worship services in her congregation at First Mennonite Church, Bluffton, Ohio. She treasures a wealth of anecdotes about what children have taught her.

She has served as registrar at Cedar Crest College in Allentown. She was also adviser to the student organization Crest Christian Koinonia. After retirement, she and her husband, a psychologist, managed a counseling center in their home, as a nonprofit Christian organization.

Love of nature keeps Frounfelker interested in amateur bird watching. She collects and presses wild flowers and transforms them into charming note papers.

Love for children has her crocheting countless mittens for underprivileged children, using yarn ends discarded by others. She has served as acting grandmother for local children during grandparents' day at school.

Love for people and for learning keeps her involved with the Institute for Learning in Retirement, at Bluffton College.

Love for the Lord and all the Lord's people, big and little, has led to Frounfelker publishing this book, *As a Little Child*.